The **Conte**

Everyone Dies for Himself Alone
Living and Dying
In Order to Keep Living

The Contemporary, DEATH

Everyone Dies for Himself Alone

Living and Dying
In Order to Keep Living

By Gabriele

THE WORD
THE UNIVERSAL SPIRIT

First Edition, 2009
Published by:

Gabriele Publishing House
P.O. Box 2221, Deering, NH 03244
(844) 576-0937
WhatsApp/Messenger: +49 151 1883 8742
www.Gabriele-Publishing-House.com

Licensed edition
translated from the original German title:
"Jeder stirbt für sich allein
Das Leben und Sterben, um weiterzuleben"
Order No. S 368en

From the Universal Life Series
with the consent of
© Verlag DAS WORT GmbH
im Universellen Leben
Max-Braun-Str. 2
97828 Marktheidenfeld/Altfeld, Germany

The German edition is the work of reference for all
questions regarding the meaning of the contents

ISBN 978-1-890841-35-5

The Contemporary, DEATH

Everyone Dies for Himself Alone
Living and Dying
In Order to Keep Living

*Death
Is the Nighttime for the Soul.*

*In the Face
of Eternal Life,
Dying Is the Soul of Eternal Day.*

Everyone Dies for Himself Alone.
Living and Dying
In Order to Keep Living

This book is for everyone who wants to find his way from fear of death to a conscious life, to security, serenity and inner steadfastness. Because, as Gabriele writes: "Whoever learns to understand his life no longer fears death."

Among other things, Gabriele informs the reader in detail about until now unknown correlations of life and death, about the condition and well-being of the soul in the various stages of dying and about what awaits a person's soul in the beyond after its physical body passes on.

A human word is a term
that can mean many things

Dear friends, throughout the centuries our society has created an image of the world for itself that ultimately is related only to this side of life, where time and space are reflected. The thinking and "living" of most people is limited to the occurrences that take place in time and space, whereby they equate "living" with the course of things in "existing," or in "being here."

In this book, I want to try to explain this side of life, that is, this "being here," so that the person who is truly seeking the truth can better understand what is contained in our human words, for example, what "living and dying in order to keep living" or "death" mean and what these want to tell us.

This is so important because we communicate with each other via language, that is, we make ourselves understood via words. However, while doing this, we often do not know whether we are understood by our fellowman, because the human language as a medium of communication transmits the information indirectly, using words as the vessel of information.

With the spirit beings in the pure Being, direct communication takes place via primordial sensations, which are, at the same time, pictures. And on matter, the life forms of nature that are not burdened by guilt – animals, plants, stones, the Mother Earth, the stars and planets, the elemental forces – come into informational communication with each other via pictures.

On the other hand, we human beings, who have moved away from the divine All-stream of love and All-unity, thus making ourselves dependent on language with all its terms, cannot at all be sure whether our fellowman has taken from our words what we wanted to express, or convey, to them.

Words are vessels, shells, which can carry a whole spectrum of content depending on what they have been filled with by the speaker, that is, what the speaker has put into the words, the vessels. This is what he is expressing in the shell of the word.

But because most individuals are not often aware of the content of their own words, nor of what lies behind their own thoughts in terms of feelings, sensations, intentions and ambitions, most of us are not capable of feeling into the words of our neighbor in order to grasp their content. So, often the words of the other person stand before us and we do not know what they are supposed to tell us. This is true of the written word as well.

This is why it is also difficult for me to take what I know, what I see in the world with the eyes of the Spirit, and what is shown to me as an inner, spiritual perception of "the beyond" that is manifest to me as the instrument of God, and to depict it in words and describe it so that it reaches the seeker of truth in his heart and in his mind. Despite all this, I will try.

Normally, we prefer to repress thoughts of death from our consciousness

As already stated, our words have many meanings; they are like expandable terms, including the words, "this side of life," or even "the beyond." For many people, the beyond is not reality, because for them it should be categorized under "questions of faith," that is, under "religion," to which the masses of people attribute an unreal, hypothetical character. To them, particularly the end of what they see as their "life," the end of their existence, death, has a slightly cold touch of something incomprehensible, enigmatic, inexplicable, perhaps even dreadful. We prefer to repress thoughts of death from our consciousness.

Sooner or later, however, the hour comes for each one of us, when we will have to deal with our existence and death, above all, when we start to deal with our past; because then the conscience particularly, often speaks with a penetrating voice, which does not always allow a good sleep.

Whoever is still young or whoever thinks that in his old age he has to engage in youthful "flights of fancy," will most likely not have calculated the shortness or length of his life on earth, if he is of the opinion that only when it has reached that point will he then want to start thinking about it. After all, who knows when the "grim reaper" will show that the hands on his life's clock have reached midnight and that his incarnation, energy-wise, has run out for him? No one knows the year and the hour. But for each one, it is certain that this hour comes and with it the question: How shall I encounter "death?" What is "death" to me? How do I feel about the whole process of my own dying? What ideas or concepts do I connect with it? Have I prepared myself for it?

Spiritual death
is spiritual blindness –
To be in a shadowed existence,
in unreality

For me as a person of the Spirit who sees the condition of all that is of the earth from the vantage point of the eternal Spirit, that is, of life, "death" is the state of a soul that has narrowed its originally far-reaching consciousness, having darkened its light through a feeling, sensing, thinking, speaking and acting that is against the law of God, which is the selfless, giving love.

Whoever denies God, the life, has closed himself to the light. He has settled into the realm of shadows, into spiritual ignorance, into unreality. He no longer perceives life as such, but is spiritually blind, that is, spiritually dead.

And so, "death" is the darkness of the soul. Whoever faces death because he sees "death" – the "end-all" of life – at the end of his earthly existence, whoever doesn't believe in a life that continues in the beyond, is spiritually dead. He is imprisoned by the external, by the earthly-material. He has covered the real life with his concepts, terms and bon vivant manners.

Since many people see death as the "end-all" of life, there are many spiritually dead on this side of life on earth and many, very many, spiritually dead souls in the beyond.

Life is a stream of inexhaustible flowing divine energy (light-power). The being of light from God is shrouded in the human being

Life cannot stop living. Life is an inexhaustible, incessantly flowing stream of light, of divine energy. No energy is ever lost. God, the all-wise One, created His children, the beings of light, equal to His eternal light-body, the eternal Father-consciousness. Over the course of eons, quite a few of the beings of light dissociated themselves from God, the Light. Through this, their light-bodies darkened.

Because the law that is God contains the free will for all His children, the Eternal granted to all beings of light that had turned away from Him and had fallen into being far from God, an earthly mantle that we call the physical body or person. This made it possible for the once pure, light-material child of God, the son and daughter of God, to stay in the cosmos of matter, on the earth, and to move about there. The human being, as we perceive him with our material senses, thus has a content – it is the being of light, which, as a result of turning away from the pure, cosmic law, is called "soul."

Through the infringements against God and, in the end, against himself as a being in the Eternal, the human being shrouded the light-filled being. The consequence was, and is, that the mantle, the person, became ever denser, that is, coarser.

The words "human being," "earth," "cosmos," "matter" unfortunately are, in turn, mere terms that call up different pictures and ideas in the individual. However, anyone who doesn't give serious thought to these realities doesn't see things as they truly are, but as he wants to see them. Through this, he kills his conscience.

God, the life, speaks to people
in the positive stirrings of their conscience.
After life on earth, no life?
Spiritual ignorance – A dungeon for our soul

When we talk about the conscience, or hear or read about it, then we have to ask ourselves: What is the conscience?

Is it a chemical reaction of the brain that expresses itself via the nervous system with the help of transmitting substances? Surely the scientists of the world have other explanations handy. But the divine, lawful, that is, positive, stirrings of our conscience come from our soul. Even if many a "know-it-all" may perhaps rebel when he hears this truth, the divine, the positive, the conscience comes to us via the soul. This is how it is. The admonisher, the divine knocking, the conscience, is the eternal Spirit, which is the eternal life. He knocks at the gate of our mind in order to make clear to us that intellectual knowledge isn't everything, but rather it is the wisdom, the life, that is important.

Many people are talented and successful persuaders when it has to do with giving excuses, terms and shoptalk. With their hairsplitting, rationalistic deductions, conclusions and erroneous beliefs, they construct a many-storied thought structure filled with nooks and crannies, in which a God and His workings not only remain unnoticed, but seem to be totally superfluous. But notwithstanding all intellectually and cleverly devised arguments about conscience, "death" and the "end-all," God is and remains existent. He is the life, the Creator of the pure cosmos, of all life forms and light beings, who also vivifies, respirates and maintains the enveloped life forms in the spheres of matter.

Whoever claims he lives only once and that, on this side of life, must then also ask himself: For what do we need our conscience then, for what the lofty words of "ethics" and "morals"? If the highest and only value is given to this "life," to this side of life, the physical existence, then why all the striving to think and live in a good, noble and selfless way? Many will say: "Well, since we are human beings, we have to impose certain ethical-moral values on ourselves." But what for – if we only live once? From the hypothesis "we live only once," shouldn't the conclusion be rather "may the stronger win"? – And for that, there's no need for a conscience!

As already stated, the conscience goes beyond the spheres that our senses can register. It is something metaphysical and comes from the primordial source of the soul, from the Spirit of God, via our soul. The conscience bears in itself the power of life. The absolute law, the divine, works through the conscience, measuring things with an absolute yardstick. This is why the conscience is for us a guide and adviser for the good – insofar as it is still intact and active. If we listen to the divine, to the pure conscience, we are led homeward, back to the eternal homeland, into the absolute, into the pure spiritual Being, from where we went forth and where we will again live eternally one day. Our soul's pathway to there goes via "the beyond," via the purification planes.

We could give many arguments against this. We could darken or even turn off our conscience with the expression "no life after our life on earth." But despite our ignorance, every person nevertheless has an eternally existing soul, which at some point has to deal with the impenetrable fogbank beyond time and space, because as a human being it had imprisoned itself in not-wanting-to-know, in the comfortable pretext, the refusal of responsibility before God, found in the statement, "there is only this side of life and no beyond."

Whoever delves into the words "live in order to keep living" and "conscience," gradually liberates himself from the dark, the nebulous and mysterious, which most people connect with "death."

For many, the word "death" is filled with pitfalls that many a one describes as the "end-all." The word "death" implies a nebulous path of suffering, sometimes even on this side of life, but most certainly in the beyond, once the soul looks into the spiral of its life.

Spiritual ignorance always means darkness, being far from the light. Our consciousness is then restricted to three dimensions and we cannot grasp the consequences of our feeling, thinking and doing. We imagine we are free and yet we are nurturing a false sense of security, because what a person sows, he will reap. On the other hand, to die consciously means to look toward the light, it means that the soul glides into the beyond, into the eternal life that knows no death, no darkness.

From fear of death to a conscious life, to security, serenity and inner steadfastness through self-discovery

Particularly during our time, when ethics and morals have merely the cut of a house of cards, the tormentor "fear" goes around bringing before our human eyes the threat of the inevitable, of death, over and over again. If we want to defeat the tormentor, we have to take up the whole question of God and of life and, in the final analysis, of our life on earth, in which every action triggers a corresponding reaction – whether we want to accept this or not. Said in a spiritual way, with our doing and not doing we are subject to the law of "cause and effect," of "sowing and reaping."

If we, now and today, were to take up the whole question of death and dying and give it serious thought, we would examine our way of thinking and acting and would watch ourselves more and more, particularly when we feel as though we are being driven or when we slip into panic because something unfathomable seizes us by the neck. If we then question this, using the analytical word "why," that is, if we search ourselves conscientiously, we will become aware of the fact that an inner power is stimulating us to self-recognition, through our soul and via our conscience. From the one who learns to listen and to sense what his conscience is advising him – for the conscience is always the good that comes from the soul – and then deals with this and from then on only does the good, fear will gradually fall away; he feels free and carried by a kind power that, from within, gives him security and a hold, and makes him happy. It is the primordial source, God.

Only when we learn to understand our existence as human beings, will we be able to grasp why we live here as human beings, and it is only then that our life begins to make sense to us. It is then that we gradually come to understand what "living and dying in order to keep living eternally" means. It is only then that we become aware of the content of the words hope, comfort, knowledge, wisdom, joy, peace, health, inner balance and beauty and will stay fresh and joyful all the way into old age. For, the one who lives consciously truly lives.

During his life on earth, the one who finds himself in the true contents of the expressions of his life, who strives to keep the God-given standards of the Ten Commandments and the Sermon on the Mount of Jesus will be plagued, tormented or pursued less and less by his own wrong behavior. He is more and more aware that a life on earth lived in a context of spiritual ethical-moral values is worth it.

A person who is willing to question himself, to explore and recognize himself in the situations of the day is a winner. His own faults and errors of judgment shock him less and less; he analyses things, makes them clear to himself, draws his lesson and moves on. The result of this is a quiet conscience, and thus, security, serenity and steadfastness in his own inner being.

He gains the experience that his life does not really depend on enjoying everything to the fullest without considering the well-being of his fellowman and his fellow creatures, but that the true quality of life lies in spiritual growth and maturity that enables a peaceable togetherness, that brings farsightedness and insight, dynamism, joy in life and a feeling of fulfillment in life.

Then we increasingly feel the current of life that carries and guides us. Then our inkling becomes certain that life is everlasting. We comprehend that life is simply life, whether here or there.

Whoever learns to understand his life no longer fears death

Whoever closes himself off from the fact that after passing away and setting aside the shell of his body, only the aggregate state changes from coarse-material to fine-material substance, is also not prepared to earnestly think about his existence or about life and to take his life on earth into his own hands.

A person excludes from his life on earth the fact of dying, of the inevitable, of death – and yet it is with us, every step of the way. It is close to us at every moment, every minute. Our birth into life on earth already brought with it our dying, for every human life simply comes to an end, called death by people. And so dying, called death, is just as natural and nature-given as our own birth.

So the question, of course, arises, why do so many people fear so-called death? Why the horror, the fear, the suppression of what happens to every person as a matter of course? Can it be that what triggers fright, panic or even helpless despair in the idea of "death" for some people is a distorted image, a product of ignorance, a not-wanting-to-know, as the result of a disparity toward life in the person? Where does this come from?

Now, during our life on earth, we could take a closer look at death and discard the fear of it.

We have to learn to understand our life and then we will also no longer fear the "caricature" of death, but find a place for it in life. Death is a difficult question only for the one who thinks solely of this side of life, but not for the one who acknowledges life as an inexhaustible source of energy and an unquenchable current of energy.

Life on earth – A segment of life that a human being can shape and use positively

We people speak too much of life. We want to live, and yet, most people do not live. As if intoxicated, they simply vegetate along without really using their time on earth in the right way.

Our materialistic world – which keeps many people imprisoned in the notion of time and space, in a purely rational and scientifically marked concept of the world or in the rut of ecclesiastical dogma – drives people, as it were, to experience many, many things on this side of life. But this does not mean that they are living! For whoever lets himself be caught up in these materialistic doings, the words "the beyond" is an expression, the contents or meaning of which is not tangible and therefore, not relevant. One simply lives. "Now," as many say, "I live." But one must learn to comprehend the term "the beyond" in order to grasp his life on earth as a segment, a phase of life and to "enjoy" it in the right way, that is, to be able to use and shape it positively.

The life, the All-energy,
floods throughout the whole cosmos.
As human beings,
we see only a very small part of it

Many scientists teach us that a human being is incapable of perceiving everything. For example, with the naked eye, we cannot see what moves in a drop of water, unless we look through a microscope. There are countless bacilli in the air and in the water that can destroy a human body under certain conditions; but with the naked eye we also cannot recognize them for what they are. Even though these forms of life are matter, we cannot perceive them without a magnifying instrument. Our eyes are not capable of perceiving the smallest forms in matter.

And so, we can conclude that much of what moves about in the material world, in time and space, cannot be recognized with the naked eye. If we were to sharpen our instruments even more, in order to see everything, if we were to sharpen them a thousand-fold, maybe even a million-fold, we would ultimately reach the conclusion that we still cannot see everything. Even our brain, which, in the end, controls us, reacts only to time and space, and for this reason is also limited in its receptive capabilities; it registers only what is a part of the world of material phenomena and at that, not all of it.

In order to grasp the beyond, we need a magnifying glass, a microscope, to observe ourselves. The instruments that help us figure ourselves out could be our eyes, our ears and our brain. If we were to take these to observe and analyze ourselves, then the questions in us would become: Who am I? and, Where do I come from?

Let us make ourselves aware of the limitations of the human being! A human being can neither make the sun shine nor make it rain. The human being also cannot create the substance of life. In order to bring forth life, he always reaches for the basic substance that already exists and is available to him.

Where does this basic substance come from, where does the energy come from that we call life? If it were exclusively oriented to the earth, then there would be no life, no energy, in all of the cosmos. Life is not oriented to human beings, either. It is a cosmic energy of which all planets are a part. Everything that we see and don't see and that nevertheless moves is life. Life is energy; it is a driving force. The functions and processes of life take place through the driving force of this energy.

In all of infinity there is nothing that is dead. Everything is energy and energy is life. And so, there must be a source of this energy, an incessantly flowing, streaming energy that brings forth the life and gives it shape in the life forms. There must be a Creator that possesses inexhaustible energy. This energy must have certain inherent characteristics, a certain order, a kind of inner structure, certain laws – an energy, an encompassing power, that orders and maintains the cosmic order.

And so, life is All-energy. Life floods through the beyond as well as through this side of life. The life that is the spirit of infinity, the All-energy, does not stop with our three-dimensional thinking that for us has meaning only in time and space. And the stream of life that we call our breath is All-energy. To breathe is not merely to take in oxygen with the air. In our breathing is the infinite Spirit that respirates all things, all living beings and the entire All. With our breathing we are connected to the All, the All-life-current.

The All-life-current, also called the All-energy, the life, knows no interruption. Life is inextinguishable. Almost every day we hear that this one or that one died. Death as such, is only a part of matter because everything that is dense, including our body, is subject to the energy of transformation. We have death, so-called by us human beings, around and with us daily.

Dying, in order to keep living in another form, is a part of our life on earth.

The process of dying – Disengaging our immortal soul from the physical body

What happens after the death of the body?
The person who has died no longer breathes. Why? Because the invisible part that we call soul has separated from the body. The soul takes with it the breath, which is the same as the life, and which it very slowly draws out of the body that is dying. This is the so-called process of

dying. With its last breath, the soul pushes the body from itself and continues to breathe without its material shell according to the law of order of the cosmos.

The process of dying puts fear into many people, because they are mainly not oriented toward the cosmic and do not think about the inexhaustible All-energy, nor do they look beyond material existence. No matter how much a person fears it, the disengagement of his immortal soul from the physical body will take place at some point in time. No one is spared this. Our soul simply is a cosmic being that is temporarily in the shell of the earth, in the earthly "spacesuit," for a certain time.

Even the term "the beyond" is suspect to many. No matter what arguments we use to dismiss the physically and rationally incomprehensible, somewhere, something is left over, for example, questions which then come up in us when a blow of fate abruptly tears us out of the often superficial and deeply rutted tracks of thought, or questions that our conscience may confront us with, like: Where do I come from and where am I going? Or: Do you really think that at the end of our life on earth everything is over and done with – perhaps through the "exhausted" energy of the Creator?

Where does the fear come from, the fear of the inevitable, of death, which is a totally natural process? The soul's thinking in terms of this side of life merely leads a person into spiritual death. On the other hand, the analysis of living in the flow of life brings us closer to dying, to an alert passage into the beyond, which is the life.

Nature does not know obliteration, only transformation

During quiet hours, many a one thinks about the where from and the where to. Whoever thinks about this will also occupy himself with the knowledge that no energy is ever lost. Nature helps us to deepen this knowledge. Nature does not know obliteration, only transformation. In all of infinity nothing exists that is rigid, static – everything flows; everything is energy. Whether it is primordial energy, the highest radiation, or low-vibrating radiation – it remains energy. The low, dense radiation is what we call matter. According to ironclad laws of order, it will be transformed sooner or later into primordial energy, that is, darkness into light, heaviness into weightlessness. As a result of this, every heavily burdened soul will become a light being, just as God beheld and created it.

I repeat: Nature does not know obliteration, only transformation. Nature is in God's hands. If God now applies this principle of transformation, because nothing is lost in His Spirit, then this also touches upon the smallest and most insignificant component of the universe. God, the All-wise, does not allow the energy sent out by Him to perish – He transforms it with His creative power.

In God, the eternal Creator of infinity, we find transformation, rearrangement and not obliteration.

A conscious life is involvement with life

Unfortunately, most people live unconsciously. We can describe such unconscious living as an existence that is tied to a certain time-span. A person brings this time-span into motion during the minutes, hours, days and months, by letting the course of the day, the course of his existence simply reel off, without himself being active to overcome the disagreeable, the not-so-good things, and without contributing to the build-up of something positive.

Is a conscious life at all possible?

To attain a conscious life, the seeking person has to first look more deeply into the eternally ruling, mighty primordial energy, into the All-energy-field that holds everything together and that, seen as a unit, flows through all things, the visible as well as what is invisible to the human eye. A person who comes to grips with the cosmic laws of the all-flowing energy and unity will also concern himself with death and dying, because life is without limit. Life thus goes beyond death.

"Death" is a word used to exclude life. To exclude life leads into unconsciousness, into the argument that, "Death is the 'end-all.' Beyond that we know nothing." And logically thinking nihilists may perhaps add to this: "Since beyond that is nothing, it's like a void." But the void as absolute emptiness as such, does not exist.

An analytical mind will analyze the word "dying" and include nature in his thoughts, for example, how a perennial plant dies, but not its roots. Dying thus challenges us to look beyond death, for God, the life of the soul, accompanies the dying one beyond death into another form of existence, into another aggregate state, into the life that is indestructible. An analytical mind will thus look more closely into the words "dying" and "living," and will at some point ask himself the question: "What is life? Am I a person who simply exists, slipping through the days without really perceiving the life that they want to bring me? Am I conscious existence? That is, am I aware during my day, in the moment? Or: What meaning at all does my life as a human being have here? Or: Do I die, in order to live? And: Do extra-dimensional and valid laws determine our life?"

Whether we want to hear it or not – every person is in an earth-school in order to come to grips with life.

And so, whoever intensely concerns himself with dying and living will also deal with the continuance of life, thus being able to better comprehend death, because he has become aware of the fact that no energy is lost and thus, nature also knows no obliteration, but only transformation.

Many people who want to taste and enjoy their existence on earth to the fullest, who do not like to accept responsibility for what they do or do not do, like the fact that they seemingly will not be called to account for the way they led their life and that they will not be presented with a bill, that is – so they think – they won't have to bear the consequences, after their demise. For them, their viewpoint that "death is the end-all" is like a protective mechanism. When part of the harvest of their seed comes to this category of people during this life on earth as effects from their causes in the form of fate, it will hardly move them to come to their senses and change their ways. For them the facts are simple and clear: The other one is to blame.

For whoever is satisfied with this protective mechanism that says that after death everything is over, death will remain a great unknown, a dark, impenetrable force.

The church institutions have given no answer to the questions on "Living and dying in order to keep living"

Living and dying in order to keep living, however, has nothing to do with the church institutions. When and where the soul will be after the death of its body is a consideration for the person alone, whose soul puts aside its human garment. The person himself is the one who determines the course of development of his soul. No last confessions, spoken into the ear of a priest or minister, will be of any help. Even the "last rites" cannot wipe away what the person has burdened his soul with. And how the life of the soul will continue after its life on earth depends on the weight of its burden, that is, on the degree of its luminosity.

The sham-Christian churches ultimately have no satisfactory answer to the following questions: Why do I live? Do I come from somewhere – where will I go to? Why am I here, at all?

Let us be aware of the fact that God is not in churches made of stone; He is not in church houses that are called "the house of God." God is the life in every living body, in every soul and in every person who breathes. The human being should be the house of God, the temple of God. And so, God is effective in every body that will again become water and earth, because nature will turn into nature again. God is the All-power, wisdom, love; He is the flowing All-law that radiates on and through every human being, the nature kingdoms, the whole of infinity. The pure Being is God, the All-law. In density, in matter, God's All-law is in matter and thus, in the density. God breathes through His creation. He also breathes in and through us human beings.

Is the beyond nonsense?
Our prejudices show that we do not have
an analytical mind

In order to become a good analyst or to stay a skillful analyst, we have to first of all learn to read with an open mind and seriously think about what we read, for example, about what is written in this book. We should first get out of the habit of rejecting the invisible as something that does not exist or that is unnatural.

Only when we have gotten out of the habit of simply dismissing the invisible or incomprehensible will we begin to think in a logical manner. What helps us in doing this is to make ourselves aware of the fact that, for example, without noticing, we are constantly surrounded by waves of the most differing kinds, yes, even permeated by them. We can neither see nor hear these waves and yet they flood through us. Why should the All-power, the stream of infinity, the life, not be able to flow through us when there are other waves of low vibration that reach us and become effective in us?

Our prejudices show that we do not have an analytical mind. For a person who can think in an analytical way does not describe something he cannot understand or comprehend as nonsense. In this way, even the beyond cannot be dismissed as nonsense. Can you prove, for example, that there is no beyond? This is why we should not show a weakness by claiming that "the beyond is nonsense!" It's true that no person can prove the existence of the beyond, but each one can come to the point where he understands that life is energy and no energy is ever lost.

Even fear, clearly analyzed, bears in itself the proof of the existence of something extraterrestrial. Fear in particular bears many indications that we tend to dismiss so lightly, like, for example, a life that continues in the beyond. Why are we afraid? And what are we afraid of? Let us learn to think analytically and to look into the complex of fear! Many a one will find in his complex of fear the intangible, the unfathomable, the nebulous, the uncanny. What is it that moves us in our inner being? In the end, it is the word of our soul to us, asking us to take a deeper look at it. This leads us more and more to an inkling that there is a superior reality that is spiritual and that ultimately is God. The reality of the eternal Spirit, the existence of God, does not open up to us because we study church history or orient ourselves to the Bible with its many contradictions.

In order to get on the track of our fear, the following could be helpful: Think about your behavior in relation to your fellowman, and include the nature kingdoms in your world of thoughts. How do you feel about your fellowman? How do you treat the nature kingdoms?

Let us make ourselves aware of the fact that what we say often does not correspond to our thoughts, and what we think, may be lined or underlaid with other feelings and sensations. This is why we can compare our feeling, sensing, thinking and speaking with a shell or a capsule. We encapsulate ourselves with what we do not admit. Consider the walnut: We do not eat the shell, but the content. It is the same with our behavior that corresponds to our encapsulated existence. It is not the shell, the capsule, that marks our body. It is not the external that goes into our soul; instead it is the respective content of our feeling, thinking, speaking and acting. This is the imprinting of our soul, and that is what makes up our character.

The content of our behavior – those things that are often not admitted but are effective in our feeling, sensing, thinking, speaking and acting, in the knocking of our conscience, in the reaction of our nervous system – are indications of what lies under the complex of fear. And think about the fact that with your many different patterns of behavior you have an effect on people and on your environment. For example, do not lose sight of what a person has to endure when you try to manipulate him, or how the environment suffers when you, as an ostentatious ego, consume animal carcasses and harm nature If you want to, compare your analysis, your repertoire of behavior, to the commandments of God and the teachings of Jesus. Examine whether what you considered right and good until now or didn't even really think about, corresponds to the eternal All-law, which is the life.

The commandments of God and the teachings of Jesus are excerpts of the eternal law, of the life that flows throughout infinity. The proof for the fact that we, every single one of us, continues to live in the beyond as a fine-material being, as a soul, lies in the actualization and fulfillment of these excerpts from the cosmic, eternal law. Our experiences with the application of the divine laws in our daily life make us free of fear and reveal to us a good, eternal life that is aware of life.

Church doctrines do not lead believers to the proof of the existence of God

Church doctrines are full of what you must do and may not do. The caption to this is: Faith alone is enough. But in time, many notice that faith alone is not enough, for faith alone does not lead to the proof of the existence of God and of the existence of the beyond. Plain inactive faith remains entwined with ifs and buts, with maybe or maybe not.

Church doctrines often teach their church adherents that faith alone is enough. This leads to the fact that many a person has turned and turns away from God because they equate God with churches and with this world and attribute injustice to God. Whoever still feels at ease in the atmosphere of his church, in the so-called church belief that brings you a state of bliss and lets you ignore the commandments of God and the teachings of Jesus, the Christ, will, when the blindfold falls from his eyes, come to the following conclusion: "God does not exist because this world is not only unjust, but horrible." The churches are simply dead bodies of power that imprison those who follow the cadaver principle that says that death is the key to life. If faith alone were enough, then God wouldn't have given us the Ten Commandments through Moses and the teachings of Jesus, which open heaven to a person if he follows them. If faith alone were enough, the Eternal One surely would have advised us, "Faith alone is enough; stay blind."

For the Church, the word "death" is an instrument of torture, with which those who made life hell for a believer devoted to the Church take the last cent out of the pockets of the dying one, whom they kept ignorant, oppressed with guilt, tormented with fear and despairing, until he wears the garment of death that no longer has a pocket. Then he is buried by the priest with unctuous words, "Lord, give him eternal rest … May he rest in peace."

Earthly law and its estimated value. God's justice applies in the beyond

The injustice in this world is the reward of the world. The unknowing and spiritually ignorant pay themselves in their own way, according to the basic principle that prevails in the world: Everything only for me, and for me only the best. This means that, among other things, corruption flourishes. The one who is looked up to is the one who has the stronger elbows, which he puts to use for his own benefit and self-opinionatedness. The opinions of those who have prestige in this world are listened to, even when they are wrong.

The courts of this world administer the law. How a legal decision falls depends on how high or low the candidate is assessed before the worldly law. The estimated value lies in the so-called scales of "justice": what the one or the other offers of value, for example, his position in society or the degree of value found in his relationships, his prestige, and so on. The legal decision is based more or less on this. However, that has nothing to do with justice, much less with the All-law of love and justice.

Another measure is used in the beyond. The planetary constellations where the soul has stored its pros and cons weigh very precisely according to the All-justice, for God is justice.

God is not the law handed down by the judge, but He is the scales of infinity. The law is terrible; justice balances things out.

41

Justice and the proof of the existence of God and of the beyond lie in the actualization of the commandments of God and of the teachings of Jesus, the Christ. No church can give us proof of the existence of God. No person, no priest, no one – we alone, every single one of us, are the proof: God's existence is in us. The truth is in us, and our eternal heritage, the power and the light of infinity – the life – lies in us. We ourselves should give evidence that God exists and thus, that our fine-material body also lives, our soul, which after the death of the body and via the worlds of the beyond, will either return to the Kingdom of God or go into a new incarnation.

We human beings get way too upset over the injustice in this world. As long as there are rich and poor, superiors and subordinates, priests, pastors and their faithful, wars, murder, exploitation of people and of whole nations as well as of the kingdoms of nature, injustice and the administration of laws will remain.

Whomever the world considers just fine, the law will be passed in favor of him. Whoever is disagreeable to the world will be served with injustice. Why does this upset us? Whoever wants to be right, no matter the price, has to ask himself what side he is on.

The structure of the fine-material soul and of the physical body

Our body is also called the coarse-material shell of our fine-material body, the soul. The coarse-material shell, the person, is marked and shaped according to the radiation of the soul. For the most part, the soul was not only once in the temporal as a human being. And so, it burdened itself during its incarnations, sometimes more, sometimes less. Light and shadow, the will of God and our self-will, are absorbed by the soul, by the corresponding soul particles, and are thus, recorded, or stored. Spoken in general terms, this is then the radiation of the soul and of the person.

The eternal, all-cosmic laws consist of seven basic forces. They are the Order of God, His Will, His Wisdom, His divine Earnestness, His Patience, Love and Mercy. If the soul burdens itself in relation to these divine basic forces, it envelopes itself in the corresponding basic forces of life. The soul particles concerned turn away from the divine primordial source of power and then radiate their burdens, their shadows, accordingly. From this, one can see that the inputs in the soul are also the respective radiations of the soul. The radiations are formed into veils, which in the beyond are the corresponding fine-material "garments" of the soul.

The three garments that correspond to the divine basic powers of Patience, Love and Mercy are light-filled veils arranged near the core of being of the soul. They are more light-filled and vibrate on a higher frequency. The other four garments of Order, Will, Wisdom and Earnestness become ever more dense, according to their burdening.

The soul garments are energy fields; they do not lie in layers over one another, so to speak, but penetrate each other, because similar burdens also lie in other garments and perhaps also become active, because the same activity has an effect on like and similar inputs in another garment.

The total radiation of the soul garments is different from soul to soul; it depends on the type and degree of burdening.

The radiation of these seven garments of the soul determines the vibration of the coarse-material garment, of the physical body, the person. The physical body, in turn, is imprinted with its essential features when a soul prepares to go into incarnation and, during its life on earth, continues to shape itself according to the feelings, sensations, thoughts, words and actions of the person.

Our earthly world is made up of the thoughts and behavior of human beings. It is coarse-material, and thus, coarse-material vibration. The physical body, the human being, is on the vibrational level of the earthly world, of matter. The sensory perception of a human being corresponds to his surroundings. The worlds of the beyond, where our soul will be after the death of its body, the soul realms, are fine-material worlds. This means that although they are not a part of the purely spiritual, divine spheres of Being, we cannot perceive them with our physical eyes.

Dangers of taking up contact with the worlds of the beyond

Particularly people who just recently received knowledge that there is a reality beyond what can be perceived physically and that is invisible to the human eyes, which penetrates the coarse-material world and can influence it, tend to apply this still limited and incomplete knowledge in practice and in thought. But in doing so, they are most probably not aware of the possible dangers connected to this. And it is not always that their reason for doing this is egocentric ambitions like curiosity or the desire to experience the unusual, thus showing off with it. Instead, it is often a simple and thoughtlessly applied "good will."

In any case, to keep you from harm, dear friends, I would like to give the following indications beforehand and within the following context:

It is neither advisable nor desirable to work, for example, toward taking up a direct contact or communication with the worlds of the beyond or their inhabitants through any kind of practices. And why not?

It is not desirable because the souls of lower purification planes, or even of the in-between spheres, are still burdened by guilt or evil of all kinds and are more or less unknowing, so that we cannot learn anything good from them or receive any pieces of wisdom from them. It is not advisable because we run the danger of being urged, harmed or even put under siege or possessed by those of the beyond who do not respect free will. Since they are poor in light, they have a need to extract strength from people. If we call up such souls, which, among other things, can be triggered by a pressing wish to experience the supernatural, then, probably, we will hardly be able to get rid of these "tormenting spirits." "The spirits that I called" – dark, earthbound souls – "I cannot get rid of" (From "The Sorcerer's Apprentice," Goethe).

On the Inner Path, which leads to God and into a life in His Spirit, we learn the following: Orient yourself only to the Highest, to God, the Eternal, and His holy law, because you will receive from where you orient yourself to. Follow His commandments and the teachings of the Sermon on the Mount of Jesus step by step in your daily life. Recognize yourself, ask for forgiveness and forgive; treat your neighbor as you would like to be treated yourself, and strive to become divine again, as you are in eternity, the son, the daughter, of infinity .

Dear friends, if you consistently act according to the good knowledge that you have, that is, if you are in accord with the true teachings of Jesus, this is how you extend your hand to Him, Christ, who stands at your side with His light, His love and wisdom. Then you will be led more and more by the good and light-filled forces of life, and you are in good hands.

From an analytical point of view,
life on earth indicates the
existence of unlimited life

We ourselves have to give evidence that God exists and that we carry in ourselves a finer substance, the soul, that lives eternally. No one else can do this for us. If you would like to, begin to analytically think through the following questions: What is a human being? Why am I a human being? Is my existence on earth my life? What is life?

So, what is the human being, as such, if we look at it strictly as a structure of flesh and bone? Taken for itself, it is a frail being that always has to be careful that something doesn't happen to its physical body. When we think of the fact that even harmful bacilli and bacteria could cause serious damage to our body or that an unexpected blow of fate could place the whole basis of our existence into question, then self-analysis would be appropriate, by asking ourselves the question or, rather, the further questions: Why am I a human being? What do I get out of caring for my body, day in and day out? Is that all there is to it? Is that the meaning and purpose of my existence, which I describe as my "life"?

If we look more closely at these questions, we inevitably come to realize that life on earth, physical existence as such, could never be all there is, that we cannot describe "life" as the fear and worry about the body and what tomorrow brings. From this realization would develop more questions that would require analysis: "Where do I come from and where will I go?" A very thorough, honest and unprejudiced, analytical self-exploration and the analytical observation of what life processes are taking place around us lead many to the conclusion that the physical body is apparently only a vessel in which something else has to be present, something that we don't see, that may even be of a finer kind of substance and that one can perhaps describe as the "bearer of life" or even as plain "life."

Whoever can think analytically will not simply claim that with this existence on earth everything is over. After all, he knows that no energy is ever lost and that energy that has taken on form doesn't simply disappear into "nothing." Radiation that takes on form also does not simply dissolve into a diffuse, flowing energy.

But it is not only by using our brain for analysis that life can give us hints of its existence. Every person also has a "heart," whereby I do not mean the rhythmically contracting muscle in the physical body.

We encounter, for example, a child. We look at each other, and suddenly it smiles. It can happen that suddenly a very special, positive sensation draws through our heart; a light, joyful and friendly feeling lightens our mood. What was that, anyway? The child has long since disappeared from our field of vision; it was simply a fleeting encounter. And yet, something touched us that cannot be categorized as material, or as matter, and which nonetheless is no less a real, tangible experience that resounds and reverberates in us. If we again think about it during the course of our day, we feel it again. In time, the impression becomes weaker, but that doesn't mean anything. Our spiritual heart was touched.

Something similar can happen, for example, when an animal looks us in the eyes, or other things. There is hardly a person alive who has not experienced a comparable occurrence, that teaches him rather impressively that there is "more between heaven and earth" than our mind is capable of understanding.

I repeat: What we don't see doesn't have to stay a riddle, a puzzle, to us. Consult your analytical brain and your heart that is near God, your fine feelings, and then you will not simply dismiss the following statements as a mystery or something that cannot be proven.

Our soul consists of fine-material substance; it is a more highly vibrating energy. Energy is life – it is not lost. Nature does not destroy itself; instead, it transforms itself. And so, there is no obliteration, instead, there is metamorphosis. The conclusion from this is that it contains life.

Let us continue to draw on our mind and our heart. Our body can be compared to a vehicle. The driver wants to be the eternal Spirit, God, who is effective in a fine-material body, which we describe as the soul. The "voice" of the Spirit in the fine-material body, the soul, wants to reveal itself in our body, in the person, as feeling, sensation and above all, as the conscience.

How often do we experience a surge of feelings, of our mood, or we have an empty or even a good conscience. Deep in this stirring is always a message for us, the person. Mostly, it is an admonishment – "Don't fall back into this old mistake" or "Don't disparage your fellowman. Why are you putting yourself above him right now?" – or even a warning – "Don't let yourself be led into temptation in this situation; you've already had some bad experiences with this!" – or a reminder of good intentions – "Didn't you decide to fully listen to your conversation partner without interrupting him? What is pushing you to break into what he's saying?" – and the like.

Often, we say that we have a "bad conscience." But we should be thankful and be glad if our conscience is alert and active. Because, seen in the light of day, the voice of our spiritually intact conscience is our good friend that wants the best for us and is constantly trying to keep us from harm.

Who is the Spirit that conveys to us the messages of our conscience? The Spirit is not the mind of the person; nor is it our witty phrases. The Spirit in our soul that sends us messages is the eternal power, the light, the kindness and friendliness, the wisdom and All-power, the eternally cosmic love – the immutable, eternal law of infinity.

Whoever counts on intellectual thinking, on the intellect, does not grasp the Spirit of infinity

And so, the Spirit is not tied to our mind. The mind is transitory; the Spirit is eternal. This is why the Spirit, the universal All-genius, cannot be rationally comprehended and studied. One has to experience it. Jesus said, *"The Kingdom of God is within, in you."* If we are ready to fulfill the laws of the Kingdom of God, then we will find the driver in us, the Spirit. The Ten Commandments of God and the teachings of Jesus, the Christ, are excerpts from the universal, eternal, immutable law, God. And so, the proof of the existence and effectiveness of God lies in the fulfillment of these spiritual laws.

If we fulfill step by step what the commandments of God and the teachings of Jesus show us, then we will feel the driver, the Spirit, in us and every little quantum of the law that is lived by us fills us again with more of His strength. It carries us upward; it radiates to us in our inner being, and the warmth of the love of God pours into our heart.

If we have oriented our way of life to the commandments of God and the teachings of Jesus, the Christ, then we have advanced so far, that we believe in the existence of the soul after so-called death. Then we are also near to realizing that there must be a divine world, which is the highest vibration, which is the law from the law of the Spirit, and thus, the creation of the Spirit, of the Creator of the eternal Being. Then, our experience is more and more that this spiritual sphere of Being is also our true Being, our true existence, yes, our homeland, where we feel secure.

With a spiritually oriented mind that is equipped with ethical-moral values, we realize that most people have turned away from their true existence, from the Spirit, the life. They have removed themselves from the All-stream, the eternal Spirit, the eternal law. With the trumpery and rubble of human intrigues and machinations, they have veiled their true existence. Even though we insist on our intellectual thinking and value it as the primary force in our world, we will not be able to comprehend the Spirit of infinity; despite analytical thinking, we will suffer shipwreck along the way.

Whoever thinks that the intellect is the same as intelligence and that the intellect is the master key that can open the locks to all rooms has not yet figured out his own helplessness.

The human being can destroy very, very much. Let us just remember his effect on Mother Earth, or think about the destroyed atmosphere of the earth and many other things. Human beings can destroy, but can no longer create order. The proof is in the pudding: Human beings are suffering, becoming ill; they are fearful of death and helplessly capitulate before their fate, and much more. The human being is also helpless before natural disasters. He goes against war and terrorism with weapons, instead of creating peace. You cannot attain peace with weapons, but only inflame further aggressions.

A person of the intellect really doesn't need to be so proud of his intellect. We recognize this when we look at the world today and see that the earth, that is, nature, gives back to the human being what the latter, in his ignorance and know-it-all-ness, in his arrogance and presumption, has sown. What he is so "proud" of is destroying our world and not last of all, the human being, himself.

The radiation of the soul marks the person.
It shows what the person has
recorded and stored

The Spirit, the eternal existence, the eternal, true I AM, is the primordial basis in every material form, even in the material cosmos and in the elements. The Spirit is the bearer of life for our body. The more we, the human being, reflect on the primordial source, that is, orienting ourselves more and more to the laws of the Spirit, the finer and more thoroughly radiated is our earthly garment, the earthly body, the person. We ourselves are the ones who determine how dense or light-filled, how heavy or light, our fine-material body, our soul, is.

And so, the more the Spirit can radiate through soul and body, the finer, the higher, so to speak, is the frequency of the earthly body. For better understanding, I want to repeat the following: The soul is surrounded by its veils, the garments. There are garments filed with more light and darker garments, depending on what we have taxed our soul with, that is, what it had to record, or store, as input. Our physical body is shaped according to the radiation of our soul, and at that, according to those soul garments that are stimulated into activity by the irradiation of the stars at the moment.

Every now and then we hear the following from people: "This or that person has a good – or less good – radiation." The radiation of the soul is, so to speak, the fluidum of the person. This is called aura or corona.

The garments of the soul – its radiation that marks the person – are in direct communication with the planets in the purification planes, where our negative aspects, that is, those things that are against the life, are stored, or recorded. These stored inputs – of the person, soul, and cosmos – form the pathways of the soul, either into the Kingdom of God, into the eternal Being, or into expiation in the shadowed regions of the spheres of the souls or into a new incarnation. Our stored inputs, light or shadow, mark us, directing and controlling us.

We human beings live in terms of time and space; this is why we labor under false ideas. Time for us means moments, minutes, hours, days and years. But time is not what the calendar shows; instead it is what we record in our souls during time, during the period of time of our earthly existence.

Because of its quicker, intrinsic movement, the soul body is much lighter than the physical body and therefore, more permeable. This brings a certain receptive capability during its life on earth, that is, we have to give the soul the opportunity to refine.

Depending on how we think and behave, certain processes take place in us that either lead to the refinement and radiation of our soul and of our physical body, or to a shadowing, whereby soul and body take on a lower vibration. The result of a lower vibration is a corresponding condensing of our physical body. Our earthly body, the coarse-material substance, is the mortal shell. The vibration of our soul with its finer, that is, more light-filled, and darker garments, shows very precisely what and how we thought, spoke and acted as human beings. And so, it can be said that soul and body are comparable to a mighty computer. What a person has entered into this computer, his person, is also stored and registered to the last dot in the central computer of the purification planes.

Where is the seat of our soul? The seat of the soul is in the proximity of the pituitary gland. As already mentioned, the ether body of the pure spirit beings, and therefore the soul that originated from there as well, is based on a spiritual particle structure. If the soul goes into incarnation, then the spiritual particles slide into each other. We could describe this process as a folding into one another of the particles. The folding of the soul can be compared to a spyglass, the segments of which, when closed, slide into each other. Whatever does not correspond to the law of God – the burdens of the human being, which can be described as more or less dark, that is, base radiation, in the corresponding particles of the soul – is the radiation of the soul and forms its garments.

The soul garments are the consciousness of the human being. In the physical body, they form themselves into the so-called consciousness centers that are arranged near the spine. The garments of the soul, the consciousness centers, stream with their radiation through every cell, every component of the physical body. The state of consciousness of the human being is the result of the radiation of the soul. The total radiation is the aura of the person.

This radiation intensity, the energetic soul garments in the body, also form, among other things, the information cord between person, soul and the corresponding planetary constellations of the fine-material soul realms, in which the inputs of the person are recorded and stored. This connecting band, which is the same as an information cord, is called the silver cord or the spiritual umbilical cord. This energetic cord is almost like a kind of pain conductor. The energetic impulses which carry the information about the good and not-so-good doings and non-doings of the person flow via this cord to certain planetary constellations of the worlds in the beyond and back again to the person who shaped and formed his soul garments through his inputs.

The garments of the soul in the beyond – A help for recognizing its guilt from earlier days on earth

And so, every person is recorded down to the most exacting detail in the beyond; our own life after this life on earth, our own individual, specific "beyond" is very near to us at every moment of our earthly existence.

For example, if inputs from the times of the Middle Ages become active, then the radiation of the soul is according to that period of time, as well as its shell garment. The active radiation of one or several garments then influence what the person hears, sees or does. Every active garment – often, only aspects of active garments of the soul – takes up contact with other souls in the purification planes or with people whose souls are presently incarnated and with which this soul still has some things to make amends for. Into the active soul garments, which, like all garments are similar to a cocoon, the soul draws all the interconnections of that time past, including the interconnections with objects to which it had a relationship back then, for example, during the Middle Ages, including buildings where people lived, with whom it, as a human being, created common causes.

The soul sees itself as a human being in the hustle and bustle of that time. It sees its interconnections with people, what it did to others and how they acted in return. In its soul body, the soul feels the suffering or the need – everything that it has caused to its fellowman of that time, but also to the animals and to nature. This experience of self gives the soul the opportunity to feel remorse for what has been stored in this soul garment or in aspects of the soul garments. Depending on the burden, in the active soul garment or garments, lies the pull toward another incarnation so that as a human being, it can repent and clear up many things that it burdened itself with and which, in the final analysis, marks the person.

Only in a few years on earth, the soul has the chance to become free from many a burden, although the possibility also exists that it can burden itself anew on earth. The pros and cons of an incarnation can be weighed beforehand with its guardian angel or with a teaching angel in the soul realms. The angel will also indicate the meaning and purpose of life on earth, as well as what its tasks would be. In this way, the soul can decide what it wants. No soul goes into an incarnation without previously receiving instruction, whether it wants to listen to it or accept it or not.

The planetary constellation under whose irradiation the soul is, takes control in the development of a new human being. Once the soul is a human being, this planetary constellation continues to be effective until, under cosmic conditions, it is replaced by another constellation. The next planetary constellation stimulates in another soul garment – or in other soul garments of another human body – whatever needs to be cleared up at that particular point in time. The new human being always closely resembles the active aspect or aspects in the soul garments from earlier times. The person himself may not be aware of this, but the way he looks and his behavior mark him.

Like attracts like.
The genes of the person are
determinant factors

It is said that the character of a person, his pros and cons, lies in his genes; these are his genetic make-up. But let us ask ourselves who is it that generations ago, perhaps even an unimaginable time ago, gave character to these genes?

When the Fall-beings – which were once light-beings that separated from God because they wanted to be like God – chose the earth as their dwelling planet and main base, and developed the human body with progressive

58

density, ever more people eventually populated the earth. Further human beings were procreated, physical bodies for souls willing to incarnate. A soul going into incarnation was and is – then as today – attracted through the lawfully effective principle of "like to like," that is, "like attracts like," by those parents who, based on their own burdens, resemble the soul in character. And so, in them are also the same or similar radiation intensities and shadowing aspects as in the soul that is preparing to incarnate. These defining, typical and individual qualities of the person are plainly manifest in the body, in the genes. Based on the attraction of like kind, the genes of parents and child are then in accord. Science, which has determined this, talks about the fact that certain features and characteristic aspects from the parents have been "passed on" to the child.

And so, it was and is the human being who "reproduces" himself in his neighbor, and who today, according to the law of sowing and reaping, can be, himself, this "neighbor," that is, himself.

The law of cause and effect, as already mentioned, is based on the principle of "like always attracts like." The attraction between two or several people, that is to say, souls, is effective until soul or person no longer is caught in the wheel of reincarnation, until the garments of the soul, which are the same as the aura of the person, are for the most part light-filled, so that they can be attracted by the Kingdom of God.

If, by wasting the life force,
the energy potential given for a life on earth
is used up faster than anticipated,
a premature death can be the result

When a soul goes into an incarnation to live on this side of life as a human being, then it brings with it its time on the earth, the length of its life on earth. This begins with its birth and ends with its demise, so-called death. The time given from birth to passing on comes from the planetary constellations that control or direct this soul. If the person does not respect the commandment of life, if he lives against the inner guidance, the Spirit, by not doing what God wills, giving in, instead, to his fits of all-too-human aspects, the person burdens himself more and more. Throughout his life's journey, he often affects his physical body violently and destructively. The result can be a premature death.

Many a soul intended to cleanse itself in its earthly garment and perhaps to even expiate some things, thus gaining more spiritual radiation power, or even beyond that, serving God and its fellowman during its incarnation. This last point can be done when the person contributes to a task that is wanted by God and takes precedence over all else, for example, a task that serves the people and the earth.

For its "life-plan" the soul has received and brought with it a certain volume of energy from the Spirit of life.

If it cannot use this force as it had been foreseen, because the person wastes it during its days on earth, the soul can weaken to such an extent that its physical body becomes sick as the result of a significant loss of energy. The causes which the soul brought with it were fortified through the negative behavior of the person, so that it may not have utilized all the time on earth intended for it, between its birth and its passing on; its volume of energy came to a premature end.

Because of accidents caused by carelessness, negligence or inattention, or as the result of exhaustion at the steering wheel of a car, an earthly death can also come earlier than foreseen, but also by a person taking in too much of certain pleasurable, addictive substances and much, much more. The causes can be manifold, but always, it is the weakening of the spiritual, or life, force of the person that lies behind this. The radiation of the soul has become so small that it can no longer support its earthly body.

Through manifold and progressive offences against the life, through the interference of people in their life on earth, by prematurely wasting the quantum of energy brought with them at birth, the danger always exists that the union of soul and body becomes shaky. This takes place via the silver cord, also known as the information cord. So if the soul can no longer care for its earthly body because of its lack of energy, then the soul separates from its physical body – simply because too little spirit power, that is, life, can flow into the physical body.

As already mentioned, a premature death of the body can be the result of the fact that the person did not make use of his time on earth, from birth until the moment of his passing.

The behavior of the person is therefore quite decisive as to whether the link between soul and body can be maintained or not.

I repeat: If the soul can no longer support the body – as the result of a severe illness, as the result of old age but also through the high-handed destruction of the body or by shattering the nervous system, the soul repels the body. The attraction is no longer ensured. The process of rejection begins – we call this death. It is nothing more than the coarse-material body falling away from the fine-material soul. If the two bodies, soul and physical body, can no longer meld together, then separation is the result.

Most people refuse to believe in these inter-relationships. They think – for example, that through sports or fitness training or by treating themselves with care – that they can postpone the passing of the body, something that ultimately is determined by nature. No person can change the law of nature. It cannot be influenced. A human being may very well be able to interfere in the law of nature, but this always happens to his detriment and never to his benefit.

It is possible for a demon to interfere in the natural body of a person if he wants to use the person for his own purposes over a longer period of time. The demon then undertakes a redistribution of energy. From his reservoir of negative energy, which he has taken from people and stored for purposes of transference, he gives to the person who consigned himself to him. In the beyond, this has severe consequences for the soul whose person let his life on earth be prolonged by the demon. The soul of such a person, who drew from the energy of the demon for his lifetime on earth, will then have to serve the demon. It may even have to go into incarnation again with a demonic task.

Whoever truly takes his life into his hands – in the awareness of the presence of God – can definitely be active and dynamic even into old age, because he has conserved his soul energies during his whole life on earth, whether by reducing the volume of his useless thoughts, by thinking about what he says or doesn't say, that is, by speaking consciously, or by being reserved in terms of excess pleasures and entertainment – yes, through his whole behavior.

However, old age can no longer gain back and activate the forces of youth. This is a part of the natural law.

The cycles of nature
show us the evolutionary course taken
on the path of life of a human being.
Life knows no standstill

Every physical body, all of matter, is subject to the cycles of nature, the rhythms and cycles of becoming and passing on. The cycles of nature show the evolutionary course taken on the path of life of human beings.

Let us begin with spring. Spring is when nature breaks forth – everything becomes green and blossoms. Early summer reveals to us the middle of the year, the early ripening and the ripening of the fruits. Late summer gives us the fullness of fruits, everything that Mother Earth is able to bring forth, in combination with the elements that work together. During the fall, the lifeblood, the power in the life forms, which in spring and in early and late summer was so creatively active, withdraws. The leaves wilt and fall off. The evergreens are surrounded by a gentle gray shimmer. Winter is – so it seems – the phase of rest in nature. But deep inside, in the roots, the life continues working, only at a more measured pace than in spring.

Throughout the year, the great master of nature is working. He clothes the earth according to the season and prepares it for the new year already during late summer and early fall. Quietly, the master of nature adorns the earth as the bride of spring. During spring, he calls to his bride. With the light of the sun, the twittering of the birds, the light, fresh green of the bushes and trees and with the gentle and colorful blossoms and flowers, the master weaves the fragrant garland of the bride and leads her into ever more light-filled days.

The life on and in the earth knows no standstill. In the great totality of the All, there is no stagnation, no back-up of the energy that is life. God never holds His breath. Life flows and streams and manifests itself and goes on and on. The Creator of infinity creates ever new suns and worlds in the universe. The universe expands unceasingly and into the immeasurable. Even on the planet earth ever new life forms emerge – gifts, children of creation of the eternal Spirit, of the life, that knows no standstill. Only the human being often does not want to fit into the process of becoming and passing by very consciously making use of every phase of his existence on earth for the purification of his soul and for the unfoldment of the true life, his eternal, divine heritage, so that after the body passes away, as an adorned bride, as a soul, to journey toward the shining gate into the eternal homeland, garlanded with the ornament of virtue and, in a light-filled garment, return home as a being of the light.

The soul of a grouchy, brooding,
embittered person who has grown old
goes to the in-between spheres
as a spiritually dead soul

What about most people? When the fall of their life comes, they turn grouchy because they supposedly missed out on much during the spring and summer of their life. And so, many an older person thinks that he has to make up for his youth and begins to act like someone in his puberty. This is often quite embarrassing for those who are close to him. Others, in turn, become grouchy about their old age and their neglected youth and do not even realize that it is through this that they actually begin to turn "old." And others take flight into illness, so that their children, grandchildren, neighbors and others may feel sorry for them. These thoughts and behavior patterns, behind which lie certain egocentric intentions, lead to the fact that an older person walks bent over, through which his eyes are more oriented toward the ground than toward heaven. This may then mean that the older person walks bent over by the burden of daily life.

But for many an older person, their daily life seems to be there for them to complain and lament about things. People who have entered their personal treadmill do not realize that particularly the fall of their life can be beautiful, if one has truly lived the various stages of his life, thus filling them with life. A person who does not master the situations of his life, who does not use nature as an example for his life, hardly shows in the fall of his life the budding of a transcendent spring. During their existence on earth, such people have not arrayed themselves with the adornment of virtue, the inner maturity, the light-filled garment.

The old person filled with grief, bitterness and resentment, filled with suffering and mourning for what he has missed on this side of life or what was not granted to him because – so he thinks – of the malice, injustice and lack of love of many of his fellow men, will truly not do well by his soul. He does not perceive the life that calls to him: Do not be such a fool! Lift up your eyes! Every day, even every hour, holds many chances ready for you; they are the fruits of life. Recognize them and pluck them by finding the positive, the good, even in what seems to be negative. Accept it! Then you will gain Me, the life, that is also your true life.

After the demise of the human body, the soul of such a grouchy, brooding, embittered person turned old will go to the in-between spheres as a spiritually dead soul. Often, such a soul is not aware that it is dead; it also doesn't know what to do with itself. This is why many souls get ready for another birth on the earth, because their former person darkened their life and did not die facing life.

Christ comes several steps toward the one who earnestly strives to change his ways

Dear friends, it doesn't have to go so far! The incomparable power of the Christ of God is available at all times even to an older person, which makes it possible for him to reform his way of thinking and living. And in the particularly merciful time in which we are now living, help over help is offered for every person, given from the fount of divine love and wisdom.

An angel of the Lord, Liobani,* gave us, for example, a revelation some years ago which was published as a book and in which she directed the following words to her older human brothers and sisters: *"However, the love and grace of our heavenly Father in Christ makes it possible for every human child to break up old narrow-minded constraints, old patterns, to give up old habits and to find its way out of the human patterns of thinking and actualize the divine laws. The Lord of Life can do all things, if the person is willing to change his way of thinking."*

Let us begin today to get rid of our old, mostly egocentric thought patterns and to direct our thinking and acting onto those pathways that the true teachings of Jesus of Nazareth set up for us. In this way, many things can still change for the good. Christ knows and loves each one of us. He wants so much to lead and help us. He comes

---

* LIOBANI, "I Explain, Will You Join Me"

several steps toward the one who earnestly makes an effort and lets himself be helped by Him, Christ.

By the way, at the beginning of the book, Liobani asks the reader a question: "Are you walking the path of joy and cheerfulness all the way into your old age?" The path is the Inner Path, which the Spirit of God in Universal Life is teaching again today. Everyone who wants to can walk this path.

The all-conscious person dies without a death struggle. Every earthly life is a gift from the Eternal to His child

As already mentioned, many parallels to our earthly life are shown to us in nature. When we watch a tree in autumn whose leaves are wilting, we will already discover the rudiments that lead life further on, small shoots for the new year. These harbingers in autumn, the fresh beginnings for the coming spring, can give us human beings hints for our earthly existence. Have we made use of our earthly life? Have we arrayed our soul with the adornment of virtue, of purity, of the light and the beauty of spring? Are we an adorned bride according to the will of God, an adorned soul, for the bridegroom who calls us in the hour of our passing? Do we hear Him, as the soul pushes away the body with the last exhalation? If yes, then the cosmic spring is granted to the soul, the light-garment, which is the journey homeward into the kingdom of eternity. Or have we clothed our soul in the garment of reincarnation? Then the first small beginnings, the small shoots in the fall for the new spring can be hints of a probable new incarnation of the soul.

Why do animals die without a death struggle, assuming that a human being has not interfered in the life of the animal world? Why does the tree, the bush, every flower die without a death struggle? Because the nature kingdoms are not oriented toward this side of life, but are one with their Creator. Why do so many people struggle with death, which in the end, inevitably comes? They struggle because they saw and see life as related only to this side of life. They cannot let go of what they call their possessions – even if it is only their existence on earth. Every death struggle is a struggle of the person with his soul. The person wants to keep "his life," which, however, is in the soul – the life of the immortal soul, which now is drawing the life, the breath to itself.

With a natural death that takes place without a death struggle, the soul can unfold without hindrance. The soul that until now was folded in on itself in the body can now unfold without great distress. During the course of its expansion, that is, its unfoldment, it takes on the form that corresponds to the active soul garments, if it doesn't linger too long in the in-between spheres. The garments of the soul can, as mentioned, also be called the garb of the soul. If the silver cord, that is to say, the information cord, has totally detached itself from the person, then not a single thread ties the soul to its mortal shell. Then, depending on the cause of death, it first stands next to its deceased body, which was, depending on its earthly age, its earthly garment, its vehicle, for many years, with which it was visible as a person among human beings. If the soul has drawn all the life force out of its discarded human body, it continues to breathe in a totally different rhythm, in accordance with its active soul garments.

During the process of death, people who have lived consciously experience how a bridge of light forms in them, which conveys to them the desire to go across it. Such a person did not waste away his life during his sojourn on earth, externalized and trapped on this side of life. Instead, he made much more of an effort to settle into the kingdom of the inner being more and more. Thus, his soul will not look to the mortal remains at the hour of death of its body, but will prepare itself to cross over the bridge, for the gentle light that grows ever brighter at the other end is the radiation of the guardian being that accompanied the soul in the person and that now continues to guide the soul to that place of life where it still has to put aside those things that stand between the kingdom of light of God and it, the light-filled soul.

With words, which are merely expressions, and with examples, I am trying, dear friends, to get across to you something of what takes place behind the wall of fog, in a sphere of vibration that most people do not perceive.

The vast majority of souls are not human beings on this earth for the first time. Instead, many souls already have several or even numerous incarnations behind them. And so, they already have been born as human beings several times and have also experienced death just as many times. But since, with every incarnation, the capacity to remember past existences is covered over, every life on earth is as if it were totally new. This is also how it should be, so that the human being can perceive the opportunities and chances of this incarnation without inhibition or without the pressure from a perhaps considerable burden of sin brought along with it. Whatever he can work off and pay back, and should work off and pay back during this existence on earth, in terms of burdens and guilt, comes toward him in "portions" through the energy of the day – always only as much as he is able to recognize and overcome on this day. Every life on earth is a great gift from the infinite grace, love and care of the Eternal toward His child.

Processes during the period of deep sleep, the "little brother of death." The "silver cord," the spiritual information cord between soul and person

Another help to find one's way to the truth is our deep sleep. Our deep sleep tells us that life knows no standstill and that after the demise of the earthly body, the soul body continues to live on another level of vibration and in another aggregate state. What takes place during our period of deep sleep could make it easier for us to learn to understand death or dying.

People who have given detailed and serious thought to death and dying describe deep sleep as "the little brother of death." When they fall asleep, many people experience a sudden jolt or jerk that goes through their body; it is as if they were falling. The shock that often follows such a feeling calls them back to a state of wakefulness. This jolt or jerk of our body is the hint that the soul in the body has loosened its hold. It wants to leave the sleeping body. If we now remain awake, the soul again anchors itself firmly in the physical body.

If we go into a deep sleep, the soul goes on a journey. According to the radiation of the soul it then goes into the purification planes, to the planets that attract it based on its momentary quality, that is, according to its radiation. This means that if the soul wears a heavy, dark garment, it will be attracted by those planetary constellations that vibrate in the lower purification planes. This means that heavily burdened souls, dark souls, remain close to the earth. On the other hand, if the soul wears a light-filled garment, then it will be attracted by more highly vibrating planets and it goes into the higher spheres of light. Whether the soul vibrates in the low or high frequency ranges, it will first move into the cosmos, of which the earth is also a part.

During its deep sleep, the soul remains attached to its body via the silver, that is, information cord. Via this silver cord, the information from the sleeping body is fed into the soul and from the soul into the body. Through this exchange of information the wandering soul feels when the person is gradually awakening.

We can compare the deeply sleeping body with a captive balloon whose air has escaped and which lies weakly on the ground. During deep sleep, the person's heartbeat, breathing, blood pressure and body temperature decrease. The sustenance of the body is turned down to the "pilot light," it lies without vigor, which means that via the silver cord the spirit in the soul is maintaining the sleeping physical body with only the quantum of life force necessary to sustain its life. The direct irradiation of strength from the Spirit, which is the carrying substance, the life of the physical body, is lacking during the period of deep sleep.

As soon as the person awakens, the soul is again in its mortal shell, the body. When we awaken, feeling strong and rested, our soul body is again firmly attached to the mortal shell.

Every now and then, our soul has difficulty attaching itself to its body in the morning. Often this lies in having slept badly, if days before we have been mulling over problems and difficulties, if we have quarreled with our fellowman or if we have a lot of physical pain. The result is that we sleep lightly, which means that the soul cannot move around in the cosmic regions that correspond to its consciousness. At the most, it can stay outside of the body near its sleeping place. As a result, it has difficulty attaching itself again to the physical body because the person is very restless when he awakens. Observations can be made about this to help us understand my explanations better.

Many of us have often had the experience that upon awakening in the morning we think: "I can hardly get up today: I'd like to keep sleeping. It's hard for me to get a handle on my body today." This means that the soul isn't totally connected to the body, that it isn't yet completely attached to the physical body. If the soul is firmly anchored to the body, we can get up without any great difficulty, and the person is again the person of daily routine.

The so-called "dead" aren't always dead. Unimaginable pain and torment for the soul that cannot detach itself from the body in time

A person who wants to put off death, the unavoidable, and yet is worried about it and moves a lot of thoughts concerning it, will now inevitably have questions like: Is dead really dead? Is there an in-between stage that cannot be fathomed? What about, for example, apparent death? Is the brain function a sure indication of whether death has become final or not?

The so-called "dead" aren't always dead. As long as the soul hasn't completely drawn its silver cord, its soul garments, out of the body, the person isn't totally dead. The mortal shell is soul-less, that is, without the energy of information, only when the soul has completely slipped out of the physical body.

75

The flowing out of the soul from the mortal shell can take place rapidly, but can also take hours or even days. It really depends on the person, on how he lived in the temporal. A saying goes: "As you make your bed, so you must lie in it." Every person decides about his life on earth himself. How he lived is how he will die. What a person experiences during the dying process and perhaps even has to endure, is something which, in many situations, the people who are standing around him cannot grasp.

If a person is strongly rooted in matter, if he has heavily burdened his soul by offending against the law of infinity, against the life, if death is the "end-all" of life for him, then at the end of his days on earth it will be very hard for him to let go, so that the soul can release itself from him. By desperately holding onto this side of life, often days longer than foreseen, a dying person holds back his soul, which is attached to the physical body via the information cord, until there is no more life force in the body, until soul and body are so weakened that a separation of energy results because a flow of energy can no longer take place.

A doctor signs a person's death certificate when the brainwaves can no longer be measured and the doctor can no longer see any evidence of breathing. However, this person can still be alive for days, because the remaining subtle streams flowing out of the soul, which are the life force that is still flowing to the dying person via the information cord – which however cannot not be measured or recorded with the crude instruments used by the doctor – still give the so-called deceased person the possibility to perceive what is going on around him. The dying person, himself, however, can no longer make himself noticed, because the soul energy, or life force, still remaining in the person is not sufficient.

The silver cord, the information cord, is, as already mentioned, also a conductor of pain. Every pain, including what goes out from the soul, is information for the body. When, for example, a person dies of an illness that caused him great pain, and when the soul has not yet completely discharged its body, then it is possible that the dying one, who has already been declared dead by the doctor, can still feel pain via the information cord, via the conductor of pain, without the apparently deceased person being able to give a sign of life. If operations of some sort are then performed on the body, for example, an autopsy or even the removal of organs, the person to whom this is done can perceive the autopsy or even the removal of organs very painfully via the conductor of pain, the information cord. He suffers unspeakably.

A seemingly deceased person particularly experiences the process of removing an organ, because the body of the one declared dead cannot be fully dead while an organ is being removed; otherwise, the organ removed would not be usable from a medical and surgical point of view. His body is kept "alive" through the use of life-sustaining instruments. These measures however, even when carried out using artificial means, bind the soul to its body, which means that the information cord, which, as already mentioned, is, among other things, a conductor of pain, continues to supply the one declared dead with life force. The one who is apparently dead can still think and feel, but no longer move. He feels unimaginable pain, but cannot make himself noticed, nor can he defend himself anymore. Unfortunately, his terrible situation is an all-too-often bitter and painful reality.

And so, the removed organ still has the life force in it – it lives, as was intended from the medical perspective. The information from the one declared dead is in the organ. This information marks the donor organ; it is the vibration of the donor. When this organ is now transplanted into another body, the latter cannot accept the vibration of the "donor" that is alive in the organ, because the donor had lived in a totally different consciousness as the receiver. For the consciousness of a person consists of the particular content of his feelings, sensations, thoughts, words and deeds and therefore, it is not in accord with the consciousness of any other person.

Thus, the recipient of the organ has a totally different consciousness. As a result, there are, on the one hand, two different planes of vibration working here, so that the body of the recipient makes efforts to reject the organ foreign to it. On the other hand, it is possible that the soul of the now deceased donor can act through its organ, the donor organ that is in the other person, via the latter's consciousness – insofar as the structure of his character offers the necessary conditions for this. This can mean that the recipient adopts part of the programs of the donor, thus going through an inevitable change of consciousness.

The one declared dead experiences similar things at the burial or cremation of his body. If the information cord that is also a conductor of pain and connects soul and body is not totally detached from the one dying, then the so-called corpse that is to be cremated or buried experiences something similarly horrible to the removal of organs. With burial, the apparently deceased person is overcome with a fearful panic of suffocating, and with cremation, it partly feels the terrible pain of being burned. And the body that has been declared dead by a doctor is kept in the crematorium in temperatures close to the freezing point until the time of cremation. For a soul that is bound to matter, this is likewise connected with unspeakable, oppressive fear, sorrow and feelings of being helplessly at the mercy of someone.

Many a one will think: "I don't believe this" or "That's a scene straight out of a horror movie!" We can say a lot in these terms, that we don't believe it or that it is a scene of horror. But we should remember one thing: Mostly we don't see what is being played out behind the scenes of our material world. Besides: Who can bring us proof that it isn't so? It would simply be one statement against the other. No one can prove to another that it is or is not so. How did the Little Prince say it? *One sees clearly only with the heart.*

The passing of a person who has lived in the awareness of God. He dies with dignity

Dear friends, we can see more with the heart, we can sense more with the heart. The suffering and pain of our fellowman and fellow creatures become evident to the fine compassion of the heart. When we open our heart, we learn to grasp and understand what they have to endure. Whoever sensitizes himself to this gradually becomes more sensitive; his "heart," his spiritual consciousness, expands, for life is unity.

The scales of his conscience weigh more finely; he recognizes more quickly in his thinking, speaking and acting what isn't good, what isn't selfless, what isn't pleasing to God, and he will no longer have difficulty reading the hints and messages for him in the adversities of his day, in the impulses from the flow of the energy of the day. Since it is important for this person to attain communication with God, the All-Spirit, he will often ask himself what the will of the Almighty is, what Jesus, the Christ, would say to this or that situation. The one who honestly asks, in order to more deeply examine himself and gain clarity over his next step, will become ever more secure in himself and independent of the viewpoints and opinions of others.

With the fulfillment of the lawful principles of God and the teachings of Jesus, the Christ, we master our school on earth, and we feel the guidance of the Spirit of God, who dwells in us. Then we no longer need to puzzle over the question of whether life will continue or not. A person,

80

who experiences in his soul what the eyes cannot see and the human brain cannot perceive and sense, need have no fear of passing on. He merely departs, which means that his soul only takes leave of his physical body, which carried the soul throughout this incarnation, and of the surroundings in which the person sojourned for some time. But life itself knows no interruption.

If Christ in us is the measure of our existence on earth, of our thinking and our acting, then the power of light and of life of the Spirit, who dwells deep in our soul and respirates every cell of our body, flows via the silver cord, that is, the information cord. And then, not only our soul garments are filled with light, but also our earthly shell, the physical body. When the hour comes for such a person to take leave of the temporal, then the information cord is already loosened to such an extent, that after the last breath of the dying one is drawn, the soul outside of the now deceased shell breathes in and continues to breathe in the beyond according to its active level of consciousness. The person is then not only clinically dead; he has died with dignity.

Such a light-filled soul will stay only for a very brief time in the proximity of its former sphere of activity as a human being, until the functions that the physical body needed to exist as a human being, have fallen away from the soul for the most part. Then it continues on its way to the eternal existence that it had begun as a human being.

The human being will become free of
his burdens only when he recognizes
his own part in his differences
with his fellowman and clears them
up with the help of the Christ of God

The behavior patterns of a person – how he lived, what he thought, how he treated his fellow men during his existence on earth – are all decisive in terms of how easily or with how much difficulty he will be able to detach his soul one day from his earthly body. Whoever thinks about these explanations will also understand the words of Jesus:

Settle with your opponent quickly, while on the way to court with him. Otherwise, your opponent will hand you over to the judge, and the judge will hand you over to the guard, and you will be thrown in prison; truly I say to you, you will not be released until you have paid the last penny. (Mt. 5:25-26)

The opponent is always the one whom we are against. The judge is justice and the guard is the scales of justice, which plumbs everything to its precise depth, the pro and con. The one who does not ask for forgiveness and does not forgive remains in his own prison, in his dark shell, where everything is stored. He will live in this encasement, in his negative patterns of thinking and acting, incarcerated, as it were, until he recognizes his own sinful part in the adversities of his existence, repents of them and clears them up with the help of the Christ of God.

Unknowing fellowmen
may perhaps cause unspeakable pain
and suffering to the dying person

An unknowing person can cause unspeakable pain and suffering to the dying person who may be struggling with death. Particularly the dying person needs special understanding from the family members who are at his deathbed.

Unfortunately, at the deathbed family members often loudly mourn and ask the dying person to say something. Perhaps they even ask him to sign his last testament, to admit where he has hidden this or that, or to still say something to this or that situation. The dying person will try to stay on the earthly plane because of such unreasonable demands from his relatives. Through this, the nerve lines of the dying person are stimulated so that using his last strength he ties the silver cord to the still present functions of the body, in order to again make himself known and perhaps even do what he would never have done as an active person. Those standing around him force him to make a statement or to sign something, which the dying person obediently does because he is not totally conscious anymore.

In the beyond and on the other side, the soul perceives in full measure what the family members are demanding of its mortal shell. This can have consequences. Depending on how the person has lived, who is now being forced during his dying hour to do what he would never have normally said or done as a human being, this soul not only remains for a long time in the in-between spheres, but it also tries using all means available to take revenge. This can come to the point of taking possession of the person who exerted influence or pressure on its dying body. The dying person was influenced by relatives at his deathbed – now the soul of the deceased influences the one or the other family member. In addition, the dying person most probably felt physical pain; by trying to influence the dying person, the family members may have contributed to an intensification of the physical pain and suffering. Such egocentric behavior patterns of family members often even prolong the dying process and contribute to the death struggle.

The desperate situation of many a soul after discarding the body

The invisible leaves many questions open. Directly after death, when the radiation of the soul has completely flowed out of the body, the soul sees its dead body lying there. For many a soul that is not only a dismaying sight but brings an alarming feeling of hopelessness. Often, the effect of this is that the soul carries out certain powerless actions like, for example, trying to waken its discarded body to life again. Despairingly, it tries to make the corpse sit up and to set it in motion. What it has to experience is that on the one hand, it no longer has the radiation power to move the material body that it had controlled until now. On the other hand, it recognizes the thoughts of those standing around, and very often becomes upset by them, because it has to face the fact that many a person, whom it liked as a human being, are actually not of good will toward it. Instead, they often exploited the deceased one during its life on earth and, through flattery and gifts, moved it to do things that as a human being, it never would have wanted to do. The soul then wants to talk to that person, but he doesn't react; after all, he cannot hear it.

We really should think about what all is taking place in the hospitals where scientific egos are being brilliant, while causing unimaginable pain in many cases to those clinically dead, for example, when an autopsy is performed or an organ is removed too soon for transplantation.

Organ transplants are approved by the churches. Whoever shares the opinion of the church leaders and their like, should first ask the church office bearers whether they, who indeed promote organ transplants, have treated their neighbor with loving care and concern, and whether after their passing, their organs may be removed, that is, whether they have made provisions so that after the death of their body, it may serve as a depository of "spare parts."

The path of every soul
is its return to the Father's house.
The discarnate soul is in another
aggregate state

The sooner we consider the subject of dying, the more consciously we will live. If we have lived according to the laws of life, if our life was shaped by the guidelines of spiritual ethics and morals, then at the hour of passing we have given our soul – and, in the final analysis, our true eternal self – freedom again.

For a spiritually awake and light-filled soul, the body, the mortal shell, is only a vehicle, so that it can graduate from the school of life on this earth with knowledge and inner maturity, that is, so that it is able to return into higher spheres of life, to the realm that lies beyond suffering and dying, because the soul can return only without its garments, without the shadows of negativity, as a figure of light to its eternal homeland, to the Kingdom of God – from where it once went out.

The path for every soul goes by way of the return to the Father's house. Jesus invited us to return home with the following words:

In my Father's house there are many dwellings; if it were not so, would I have told you that I go to prepare a place for you? And when I go and prepare a place for you, I will come again and will take you to myself, that where I am you may be also. (Jo. 14:2-3)

And He further said:

Come, O blessed of my Father, inherit the kingdom prepared for you from the foundation of the world..."
(Mt. 25:34)

Because this is the path for every soul – no matter how often it may still strive toward the material garment, toward incarnation – at the deathbed of our neighbor it should be clear to us that every process of dying is an important and significant station on the way home for this soul. No matter whether the soul slides into the worlds of the beyond gently or whether dying is a struggle with death for the person, that is, a death struggle, we should behave calmly and reverently at the deathbed and be aware of what the dying one now has to go through.

Where is the soul when it has released itself from its mortal shell? Is it alone? Or who is with it?

If the soul has totally detached itself from its mortal shell, it finds itself in another aggregate state. It has a form, a shape, that is similar to the human, but its substance, its consistency, so to speak, is finer and lighter.

To understand the other aggregate state better, let us briefly bring our world to mind. Our world, which we call matter, is nothing more than low, dense radiation. The denser the material radiation becomes, the heavier is the material substance, the matter. And so, the aggregate state of matter is a low radiation, a coarse, dense substance. The human physical body is a part of this. Matter as such cannot penetrate the finer worlds, and this is also why a person cannot see them. On the other hand, the finer substances, that is, the soul in a higher aggregate state can see the lower radiation and penetrate as far as it is possible for the active shell-garments mentioned before, according to the principle that like vibrations attract, in turn, like vibrations and flow through them.

However, our soul – even as a human being – is in communication with the planetary constellations which have registered and stored its shadowed sides via its garments, its shells, that can be compared to a cocoon.

As mentioned, immediately after the death of the body, the soul usually stands next to its body. It can send to it, irradiate it, so to speak, perhaps even still radiate through it if it is still warm, but it can no longer move it nor express itself through the dense material, the body, that is now deceased.

The soul reviews its life on earth.
On its own body, it feels the pain
that it caused to others

In this situation, the soul reviews its life on earth, which has now drawn to a close, step by step, that is, picture by picture. The soul, which very gradually slid out of the mortal shell, perceives what is recorded and stored in its fine-material shell, which surrounds it and is active in its radiation.

Every soul garment consists of countless sequences of pictures, that is, inputs or records from its human past. These are the inputs of the person that have been recorded in the soul and in the corresponding planetary constellations.

After leaving the body, the soul looks into its active soul garments and sees some of its deceased relatives. It sees them as it saw them when it was a human being, people from the past and who perhaps greet and welcome it into the other world – depending on how their relationship was, it to them and they to it.

But the soul can also see former human beings whom it had wronged in the temporal as a human being, for example, whom it had cheated or robbed or even murdered. Or it looks into the slaughterhouses where, as a person it had murdered animals in the most terrible ways, preparing their bodies, the meat, for sale. Or it sees itself as the keeper of the slaughter animals in factory farming, where as a person it kept these animals in the cruelest of ways, feeding them food that was not appropriate to their species, in order to then sell them as an expensive commodity, as an animal for slaughter. The soul sees itself in the woods where as a person, as a hunter, it wounded animals and killed them perfidiously. Via these and other active pictures, the soul feels the first painful experiences, the pain, which, as a human being, it had caused to people and animals.

Everything that the person thought and did against the law of life, the soul will feel on its own body. Even when the person incited others to murder people or animals, or when he tortured animals for experimental purposes in laboratories or acted against the life in agriculture – as a soul it will have to experience all this martyrdom on itself.

As a soul, victims of violent acts seek out those guilty to take revenge on them

If a soul has been thrown from its body, for example, in a car accident or if the body is destroyed in war through bombs and grenades, or if the person was killed in ambush, the soul often doesn't know where it is and what happened to it. Many of these souls still feel they are human beings, until very gradually it dawns on them that they no longer are a human being because they no longer get an answer from people they ask questions of and aren't perceived by them at all. Such an awakening of a soul in the beyond can be quite a problem, because it wants to have a body again, no matter what. Its life on earth was violently taken from it, which can lead to serious disturbances in its soul garments, and to the most urgent desire to incarnate again as soon as possible.

Frequently, such a soul doesn't leave the earth for a long time. It remains among those people who, according to its point of view, are guilty or at least partly guilty for its physical death. It then uses the soul power still available to it to influence and take revenge on the people who have sent it into the beyond. If it is possible, the soul directly clings to its victim. So it can be that the role of culprit and victim is reversed: The culprit abused and killed its victim – now the culprit becomes the victim of the soul, which clings to him in order to take revenge on its tormentor and murderer.

Even when such a soul was flung from its body through the detonation of a bomb, it looks for the one or more perpetrators of the deed, to take revenge on them. It may even follow the trails that lead into the highest ranks among the people, to the commanders and even individual proponents of war.

Souls send out their frequencies.
They can influence people who have
the same quality of radiation they do

To understand better what goes on behind the fog bank, beyond our capacity to perceive, the following point of view can be helpful:

We human beings live in an ocean of vibrations of the most differing kinds. Countless frequencies surround us, such as frequency wavelengths of radios, televisions, computers, telephones, cell phones and long range walkie-talkies. Everything that is energy goes out in sending and receiving waves. Even our feelings, sensations, thoughts, words and actions are energies, waves that seek out their receivers. All of infinity is oriented toward sending and receiving, the highest radiation of infinity as well as low, dense radiations. The radiance of the stars, for example, is energy, and thus, waves. Even those who are discarnate, the souls, send out their frequencies. We human beings cannot see the waves that surround us and often cannot hear them, either.

The programs of the human being that are stored in the brain and control the whole person consist of his repertoire of feelings, sensations, thoughts, words and actions. The person sends out unceasingly according to these programs, and also receives according to what has been sent out. As a result of this, the human being is a sender and, at the same time, a receiver. Our sending potential corresponds to what is stored in our brain. It is our sending and receiving equipment. According to these programs, we can absorb all those wavelengths, all those energies that are present in our sending and receiving capacity, that is, that are like our own sending and receiving potential.

What is possible for a person can also be done by a soul that has the programs of its former person stored in its soul and in its enfolding garments. For example, a soul that is still moving around in the in-between spheres, that is, which is still very close to the earth, can affect and influence those people who correspond to its wavelength. This means, the soul can influence living physical bodies that are of the same kind of radiation quality. But it can no longer control its own dead body because after the soul flowed out of it, the body is subject to decomposition into the corresponding components of the earth.

Souls that stay near the earth
move about in the pictures of their past.
Many a soul possesses or besieges
human beings in order to live out its
world of desires

A soul that is close to the earth and which cannot come to terms with the death of its body, thus lingering among family members that mourn it, at some point has to painfully recognize that they no longer hear it.

The "living" talk about the so-called deceased and do not notice that the waves, the words of the one whose soul was uprooted from its body, reach their ears, for example, the words "I am living!" They talk about it as the "deceased" one, and yet, it lives! The waves from the soul that reach the ears of the family member are no longer perceived by the latter, because the "living" concern themselves too much with matter, with the dead and dying, instead of with the life that knows no standstill.

Because of their ignorance, matter is all that counts for many people; they think and act, for example, according to the motto, "I live now – afterward the deluge can come!" It is quite possible that the person whose soul is now discarnate also thought the same way and is now lingering in the in-between spheres. The "deluge" of being forsaken and the sudden knowledge that it, the soul, lives, seems to plunge many souls into extreme need, helplessness and despair; they are completely at a loss.

Many then cling to their active soul garments, in which a part of their past is recorded, that is, that part that happens to be active at the moment. They live in this garment, which is like a cocoon; they live in the pictures of their past. Their family members, their relatives, are also in this cocoon life. Pictures from its past are recorded in this cocoon, pictures of its youth and of its middle age, pictures that show a life on earth in all the different facets of daily living. Many souls that are close to the earth move about in these, particularly if, as a human being, they were concerned only with themselves, with their desires and wanting.

If the imagery in the cocoon is not sufficient to more or less satisfy the soul, then many a soul seeks a channel through which it can live out its world of desires. If it has found a person who has similar predispositions as itself, the soul tries to influence this person in order to live through him. The human being in question is then "possessed" or "besieged."

Particularly in our world, where ever more people devote themselves to materialism, that is, who live out their existence in externalities, such attempts of a soul to attach itself to a person are not seldom. Many a soul is successful at this.

There are people on this earth on which hang clusters of low, earth-bound souls that have no other intention than to taste, via the human being, those energies that served it during its own life on earth toward its lusts, its intoxication, and toward the satisfaction of its passions, drives and addictions of all kinds.

The breath comes from God.
He is the life of the soul and of
the mortal shell. After the person's last
exhalation of breath, the soul continues to
breathe in another rhythm

Most people repress thoughts about death and dying. It is foolish to repress what is a part of us and of our life on earth – the hour of passing. Dear friends, at some point in time, each one of us will stand before the threshold called dying. Wouldn't it be better to deal with it in time, before we slide out of our body at a certain hour "X" and fall into the unknown, filled with fright?

Since no energy is ever lost – where does the energy of our body and of our breathing go after the death of our body? We could protest and say: "The earthly body is from the earth and goes back to the earth. But what about our breath? Is this from the earth? If yes, then the earth and its nature kingdoms must also breathe like we do. But they don't have our kind of breathing. So, where does our breath go?

The nature kingdoms breathe in very long cycles, a human being, in short rhythms.

Book learning in a life on earth has given us a whole range of plausible explanations about the breath and the process of breathing. One of them, for example, says the following: Breathing is a physical process. When a person stops breathing, he is dead. So according to this statement, the breath is not something tangible, nor does it belong to the earth, instead, only the body does, without its breath.

Another interpretation would be that through its breathing the body takes into the lungs the oxygen that it needs to live. From there the oxygen goes out into all the organs and cells of the body via the blood stream. And so, the breath draws the air, a mixture of gases, into the physical body which takes oxygen from it and then expels the left-over components of the air, which is called exhaling.

Thus far, some aspects from book learning. The divine law, which is eternally valid throughout the whole universe, which is effective throughout the pure heavens as a stream of light, and which determines all life processes in matter, on the earth, in human beings and in nature, however, does not orient itself to "book learning." From the divine wisdom we can say the following:

Breath is life and God gives it to the soul and to the human being. Who can prove otherwise?

All the external, physically noticeable processes like air, oxygen, lungs, blood, etc. only relate to matter and are a part of the functions of the human body. But in the very depths, in its spiritual core, something else is effective: It is the eternal Spirit, which alone is the life, and which alone can give life, let it flow and maintain life. The Spirit of God, that is, God, Himself, His breath, respirates the human being via the soul, also via nature, thus giving him life during his time on earth, when the physical body, the "human being," serves the bearer of eternal life, the soul, as a vehicle.

Everything that comes from God, as, for example, our breath, which is the life of the soul and of the mortal shell, the human being, goes back again into the Spirit, into the life. The Spirit, the life in the soul, takes the breath into itself via the soul and after the person has exhaled his last breath, the Spirit lets it flow into the soul in another rhythm. This means that after the last breath of the human being, the soul breathes in, and continues breathing in another rhythm.

If a person on this side of life occupies himself with the beyond, and if he has applied the cosmic laws of love for God and neighbor in many details, then the person will die in dignity and awareness, when the hour has come. The soul will flow out of the mortal shell and be received by light-filled beings, which accompany it into those zones of life, those planes that correspond to the present level of consciousness of the soul. Then the soul will be among the beings that are similar to its nature.

How a person shapes his existence
on this side of life determines
the life of his soul in the beyond.
Its guardian spirit and other light-filled
beings support it in word and deed

The one to whom it was important to progress spiritually on earth, that is, to grow in closeness to God and unfold the eternal being that he is in his innermost being, will also find good conditions for his further spiritual development as a soul. His guardian spirit and other light-filled beings will support him in word and deed.

Even "over there" there is "continuing education" in spiritual schoolings for the souls, which as human beings also visited the spiritual schoolings of the Spirit of God, treasuring them and following them for the most part.

Many a person, who still claims that he followed the Inner Path, may also have to realize as a soul that on this path he may have turned his back on a number of possibilities – perhaps even many – for self-recognition and thorough purification, for even in the purification spheres spiritual guidance is given. The soul may then not find itself in the more light-filled spheres, as the person may have dreamed of, but the willing soul can be sure of finding help no matter where.

Whoever has already become accustomed to and practiced in relating to himself all hardships that hit him, and in seeking the causes for unhappy experiences in himself instead of in his fellowmen has a great advantage in the soul realms, namely, that those still open aspects of guilt in him don't necessarily have to lead to longer periods of expiation. For the remorseful sinner who has recognized himself and wants to clear up his guilt with Christ, His Redeemer-spark is available – here, on this side, as well as in the beyond. However, these processes cannot be surmounted as quickly in the beyond as they can here on earth.

Dear friends, even when the one or the other soul is bitterly remorseful over the lost opportunities of its incarnation, even when the sense of "too late" flames up and burns painfully in it, the purification planes are a part of the path home into eternity for the soul. To know this can be a certain help for the soul, a help toward hope and confidence and the motivation to exercise the necessary patience over and over again.

From the descriptions given until now, it is clear that those souls among others are particularly in bad shape, which, as human beings, either knew nothing about the spiritual reality or didn't want to know anything about it. Whoever does not include the ethics and morals of the teaching of the Nazarene in his life will usually create more causes, that is, will inflict more burdens on his soul than he is aware of. Why? He doesn't know himself as he really is because he deceives himself on the content – that is, on the true value, the actual quality – of his own thoughts, words and actions. In this way, he leads a life filled with façades, which, in the end, is untruthful. Since the lack of honesty toward himself silences his conscience more and more, this person may come to believe that he is a good, decent, well-meaning person of noble character – until at the hour of death, he is unavoidably and, in the end, unquestionably confronted with himself, with the true picture of his character, or his lack of character ...

A shadowed soul that feels bound to matter, because as a human being it lived oriented only to this side of life, will also be taught by a light-being, which, however, is often hardly perceived by this soul. The soul may look into its active soul garments that surround it, into the mirror of this side of life. It is the review of its life on earth, which we already referred to earlier. Through this, the soul should become aware of how much time, that is, energy, it wasted as a human being, for instance, through unimportant, egocentric things; it should recognize and grasp what was right and wrong during its existence on earth, how much suffering – often unknowingly through its egotistical behavior – its person caused to other people and how wickedly it may have treated nature and the world of the animals during its existence on earth. The soul sees and experiences on its own soul body the suffering endured by the people and the animals through the person it once was, and it feels the pain of the animals whose torturous death it contributed toward by consuming their meat.

Everything, absolutely everything, is recorded. No content of a feeling, sensation, thought, word or behavior of a person is lost. Everything that is negative, that is not soon cleared up, the soul absorbs into its spiritual particle structure, its soul garments, which form its radiation. What the soul has stored is also recorded in the corresponding planetary constellations. The following is written:

Are not two sparrows sold for a penny? And not one of them will fall to the ground without your Father's will. But even the hairs of your head are all numbered ... (Mt. 10:29)

This means that energetically speaking, no stirring on our part is ever lost.

If a person was a prisoner of this side of life, if he exclusively related to this side of life, then the inputs of the soul will stimulate him to incarnate again – either to continue in the temporal as before, out of stubbornness, or to indulge in its hatred of people during its earthly existence, or to improve itself as a human being and to finish the school of earth with inner success.

The specific task of a soul for its existence on earth. "Whoever doesn't want to hear must feel"

Every person has his particular learning task, which his soul brought with it into its existence on earth. Who tells us what our task is? Our day tells it to us in many different ways.

It is our conscience that speaks to us. It is the qualms that call our attention in our solar plexus via the central nervous system. It is our agitation when we don't like something. These and many more are signs that the soul wants to convey a message to us. However, what helps us above all are the commandments of God and the teachings of Jesus. If we compare our own behavior to the will of God, then we know how we should think, speak and act.

When we think of the fact that we ourselves create our own well-being or sorrow, how true is the following saying: *Whoever does not want to hear must feel.* Whoever takes this saying literally – or the statement of Jesus in the Sermon on the Mount, *"Do to others as you would have them do to you"* or said in a different way, *"What you don't want others to do to you, do not do to them"* – will not cling with all his strength to this side of life as do many a one who throws all impulses to the wind with the excuse that they live only in the temporal, and at that, only once. Such a point of view makes a soul heavy, which, after the demise of its earthly body, then orients itself earthward and wants to stay near the earth after its last hour, remaining there for a long time.

The person can no longer change
the condition of his soul at his hour of death.
What applies is: light or heavy?

Many a person asks himself the following question over and over again: "Why do I have to endure or suffer through this?" Or: "Why is dying such a torment for some people?"

We can better classify the fate of a person under the viewpoint of how heavy or light is his soul. How the separation of the soul from the dying body of a person proceeds depends on how light or heavy it is. The person himself creates his own light or heavy soul through the goals that the individual takes on for himself. The more consciously a person strives toward a spiritual direction, a higher goal, according to spiritually ethical, moral values, and fulfills these little by little, the lighter will his soul body, the soul, become. The baser our behavior and striving is, the heavier our soul.

We don't need any experts, theologians or psychologists to help us figure out the degree of lightness or heaviness of our fine-material body. Let us monitor ourselves: Troubled, negative, fearful thoughts, thoughts that are alive with greed from extreme or egocentric desires, envy or resentment, oppress us. Even worry and fear about our own well-being and our future make not only our heart heavier, but our soul as well.

The opposite of being heavy is being light. For example, when we are in harmony with our neighbor, understanding, caring, positive thoughts, confidence and hope make us buoyant and light. And above all, when we rely on God, entrusting ourselves to Him in pain and suffering, our heart and soul body will become lighter.

When we pay attention to the language of our conscience, which sends corresponding signals via our body, we will ourselves feel where we stand, that is, what kind of person we are. When we monitor ourselves, we are our own best psychologist.

We can compare the state of our soul with a drop of water. When it turns into steam, it gets lighter and takes on a finer consistency. Gases of all different types can also be examples that help us become aware of the difference between a finer and lighter substance and a heavy one. Every density that is intensified by our negative behavior, by our turning away from God, ultimately has its effect on our soul.

Every person who is against nature and the animal kingdom, who contributes toward burdening the earth, for example, through bombardment during war, by burning forests, building dams, by robbing the land – here, this means to take the land from the animals – or by shaking the earth in many different ways, becomes guilty before the Creator, before Mother Earth and before everything that is above, on and in the earth. Through this, the soul of such a person is heavily burdened and it becomes heavy; the soul garments turn dark and dense – the soul has become earth-oriented after its physical body has died, such a soul is close to the earth, tied to the earth.

A soul that stays on and near the earth after it is discarnate is unfavorable not only for those people that come into contact with it and are spurred on by it to further unlawful acts, but also for the soul itself. How?

Since it does not go to that place in the soul realms that corresponds to it, where it could and should improve its radiation through a process of purification, it is not possible for the soul to work toward its spiritual progress. With its earth-oriented doings, the soul does not continue to develop further, that is, upward; it does not go a single step forward on its way back into the eternal homeland.

After death the following criteria is inevitable: light or heavy? We can no longer change the condition of our soul at our hour of death. As a human being and as a soul, we are whom we have become during the course of the years of our incarnation through our feelings, sensations, thoughts, words and actions.

Dear friends, we are still human beings on this earth; we can still use the time. We can begin right now, without wasting time. While reading this book it could be that something has rung a bell in the one or the other, a stirring could have been noticed. Who knows – perhaps for many a one this is a chance to improve the radiation of the soul, to help it toward a bit more lightness?

One thing is for sure: Christ is always present. He is near and reaches out His hand to you, in order to help you. And God, our eternal Father, radiates courage and His almighty power to every person. Let us use the time, dear friends! Let us use the day; let us use this hour!

"Heaven" and "hell"
are states of consciousness of the soul
that the person himself has created

As already mentioned, the active soul garments correspond to the state of our soul. It is attracted accordingly by a planetary constellation or remains for a long time in the in-between spheres, that is, near the earth.

The soul will be with the same kind of souls, like-minded souls, until a change takes place in it, until it has felt remorse for its dark sides that are against the light and clears these up – as far as this is possible in the beyond or from there. Such places of residence, so to speak, can be "hell" for many a heavy soul. On the other hand, for a more weightless and light-filled soul, the more highly vibrating spheres could be a "pre-heaven."

Let us be aware of the fact that "heaven" or "hell" are states of consciousness that we create ourselves. Every person determines at every moment his level of consciousness, which I would like to describe as "hell" or "pre-heaven." However, no soul will remain eternally in "hell" or in "pre-heaven." The pathway on which Christ, our Redeemer, goes with us is the pathway into the eternal Father's house, into the Kingdom of God, into the eternal light, from where our pure body of light went out.

Earth-bound souls influence
and manipulate human beings;
the atmospheric chronicle is pouring down.
Whoever does not develop higher
ethical-moral values
often remains a controlled person

I repeat: At the moment in which the connecting cord, the silver cord, the conducting, that is, information cord is cut off from the physical body, from the person, the soul body rises or falls. If the soul is very earth-heavy, this says that it is strongly attached to its earthly works, that it is deeply rooted in the earth, which includes being tied to its wealth, its goods and certain people. It is possible that this soul remains close to the earth for a very long time, as is often the case. It is such souls that are called earth-bound souls.

Also such things as hatred, animosity, revenge, envy and many other things bind the soul and keep it attached to the earth. Then, no kind words will help, not even from a light-being, to see the whole thing in the law of justice. These unknowing souls are as if "deaf" and "blind." Their consciousness is, to a point, considerably narrowed. Driven by their concepts and desires, they press toward the quickest possible incarnation, that is, to becoming human beings again, preferably in the same family or the same interest groups, offices or institutions, even in the same villages or towns. Or they strive toward being near a hellish sphere of influence on the earth where they can pick up and continue where they had left off before.

In many villages or towns, for example, the inhabitants are at enmity with one another, and at that, beyond death. Where will such souls linger? On the one hand, they will continue to linger in the villages or towns. On the other hand, they take the next possible opportunity to incarnate in the same communities, if possible, in the same family, in order to pay back the others for what they supposedly had done to them.

Whether the person whom they intend to take revenge on is still present in the temporal, does not worry such a hate-filled soul – they want to take revenge, "into the second or third generation." Whatever is raging in them drives them on a rampage.

Earth-bound souls often remain as souls among people for a long time. They hang onto people; and so, they lay siege or possess these people and stimulate them to certain negative actions by using all the negative and all-too-human tendencies, existing in them for their own insinuations, manipulations and control.

On a small scale, the same things can often be observed in terms of their effects and repercussions in the private life of an individual, as well as on the large scale of world events. The negative forces, the opponents of God, put all their available means to work to darken the light on the earth, in humans and in souls, and even – if they only could – to extinguish it. They use every possible opportunity that presents itself, to bring about need, suffering, cruelty, war, death and chaos, and to drive people into further externalities, pushing them into aggression or apathy.

Many a power-crazed person of this world seems to act under his own volition, when he makes decisions that may have disastrous and far-reaching consequences for the fate of a whole nation or of many, many people. In reality, he is operating under control, as the accomplice of invisible darklings, as a marionette without will, that carries out what his "backers" have input into him.

Since the emergence of mankind, many of the energies produced by human beings have accumulated in a certain layer of the earth's atmosphere, where they form a kind of "depot" for all kinds of information, one could call it a chronicle; in general terms, one calls this chronicle of mankind the ether chronicle, or the atmospheric chronicle. It contains – aside from the positive, which people have put into it through their God-pleasing thinking and living – the collective potential of all the causes of mankind. These are the causes which until now have neither been expiated nor have they come into effect.

But since the Christ of God radiates powerfully into this time, the great time of change toward the era of light, because He is building up the Christ atmosphere – through His holy word and through what is taking place on the earth truly in His name and with His power of love, kindness and wisdom – the atmospheric chronicle is very gradually dissolving. Of course, dissolving in the sense of disappearing or being absorbed is not the case, for no energy is ever lost – as we so often say. It is pouring down, so to speak.

The causes pour down onto the perpetrator in the form of corresponding effects, that is, as fate. Many inhabitants of the earth, many people, are hit by this.

The negative energy potentials that roam about in the atmosphere act like entities. They want energy to fortify themselves with; they send out their vibration, their frequency, and seek their corresponding receivers according to the principle, "like to like, like attracts like." In this way, the same kinds of thought powers come together and influence mankind. The aura of the world is dark, particularly at certain times and in certain areas, through the dark energies that find the milieu that corresponds to them.

Because the atmospheric energies are constantly lying in wait to set off and intensify the same kinds of things in us, many people are controlled in many different ways through their still present egoistic tendencies, through their wanting, their intolerance and arrogance, their bad habits and weaknesses. Whoever lets himself be influenced will stay controlled in manifold ways, until he sets out to honestly recognize himself, to take the shaping of his life into his hands, conscious of his responsibility, and to build up higher ethical-moral values, so that at the zero hour, he may enter the life. In any case, what holds true is that the countdown has already started long ago.

Dear friends, why am I writing about all of this? Well, whoever knows the dangers, whoever knows about them can better see through and classify many a thing. Then, he

110

can draw his conclusions from this knowledge and find his own way. The one or the other will surely come to the conclusion that in the end, there is only one way and it is namely: "Nearer, my God, to Thee!" And he will strive to settle into the kingdom of the inner being and be safe there.

During the day the person decides what his "afterlife" will be like

Dear friends, whoever now thinks that it is time for him to think about death, I would advise him to first take a good look at the content of his existence on earth, his feelings, sensations, thoughts, words and actions. For from the hidden, often not admitted negative content of the expressions of our life, the garments of our soul are formed. This will be assessed in the "beyond," because as the tree falls, so will it lie. Only when we explore our life on earth and thoroughly analyze our character traits, will we more or less know how we will die and where we will be as souls.

Our life on earth always runs its course between two poles: before and after. Our days lie in-between, and are important and decisive for us because every one of our days throws its light onto aspects of our base self, so that from there, we can attain our higher self, a more light-filled soul. Our life before fits into our today. Each day brings a quantum of our life before, "the before," with it. Each day, we can also decide what our "after" will be like, for the day always comes as a good friend, who supports

111

us to shape our soul with more light. Whoever doesn't accept the day makes of it an enemy. For whatever a person again gives back to a fading day to take with it as unresolved negativities – causes from our past, from the "before," as well as further, new negativities of hatred, envy, animosity, strife, indifference and much more – a future day will bring into the arena again in another way, but then, perhaps, as an effect, maybe as illness, need, blows of fate or even a premature death.

The life-film rewinds. The forward run takes place until 40-48 years of age. Building the matrix for the next incarnation

The rhythmic "life-film" of every person that can be compared to a film reel begins at birth and ends with the death of the person. Until a certain point in time, which can be different for each individual, but normally runs between 40 and 48 years of age, the life-film of a person, runs forward, as it were. It is storing and saving. After this point has been reached, the life-film stops for a short time and then begins to run backward. The reel of film is being gradually rolled back up, so to speak – the life-film is running backward.

During this rewinding process, the person growing older is being shown via impulses from the energy of the day, what he has stored or recorded in his past during this incarnation. At the end of each day, this part is closed; another piece of the film is then rolled up.

Another way to illustrate this process would be a papyrus roll. With the birth of a child it opens and unrolls bit by bit until the aforementioned point in time, which normally lies between 40 and 48 years of age in the life of a person on earth. During this process, new aspects from the person's way of thinking and living, from his pros and cons – that is, further burdens by way of guilt or infringements against the laws of God, but also by removing present shadows through purification – are entered along with the already present records. The roll now rests briefly and then will be rolled up again successively following the rhythm of the person's days on earth.

And so, "life going backward" signals that we are growing older. If during the forward time we shaped our character, we can recognize it now during the rewinding phase and draw corresponding conclusions, which gradually make it possible for us to recognize a part of our negativities and to make amends for some things with the help of the Almighty.

During the time of birth to that point in time when the life-film begins to run backward, which lies between the ages of 40 and 48, it is possible that the person will create his next incarnation through new burdens and by not working off the already present burdens. An incarnation is put together in the material cosmos; it is like a matrix in which all the character traits of a person, his blows of fate, all his good and less good deeds, all behavior patterns that will come to light during the next sojourn on earth, are all recorded. If the soul is light, that is, burdened only very slightly, then its "matrix-person" – this is how I would like to call it – can be dissolved in the beyond with the help of the Spirit of God.

But if the deceased person was very oriented toward the material, the soul has a certain heaviness about it, and this is also how the incarnation-matrix was formed, which tends toward the earth, and thus, the soul, as well. If the soul has again incarnated via its matrix, the result is a new person who fits the inputs from his previous existence. Now, it depends on whether the new person orients his life on earth to the divine laws or violates them. From his negativities a matrix can form again, which, in turn, points to another incarnation.

It is important for every person to know the following:

The rhythms of life during our existence on earth up to the age of 40 to 48 years are decisive for our development as a soul and perhaps even for further incarnations on earth. During this time we form our character and thus enter all the contents of our feelings, sensations, thoughts, words and actions into our soul and into the corresponding planetary constellations.

While the life-film is rewinding, which reflects to the person everything that he has already entered during the forward phase, the person growing older can improve his cosmic matrix by recognizing, repenting and clearing up all his wrongdoings; but he can also intensify his nega-tivities, whereby the new burdens, however, are not as severe as they are during the forward phase.

Whatever is present in the matrix-person is also stored in the soul and in the planetary constellations. Every person thus builds his own future physical housing, which, during his lifetime, he sets up according to his moral conduct on earth.

Dear friends, we should recognize that everything that befalls us, whether positive or negative, is good for something and can serve toward the best if we work out the positive in the negative, affirming it and clearing up the negative. Whoever builds up the positive forces by acting in this way has the key in his hand and the tools to truly live. With this knowledge he can overcome spiritual death.

God brought the inner religion, the religion of the heart. It makes an external religion superfluous

Many people bind themselves to "religions," thinking that their religion's teaching is the divine measure for all things, that their religion is the way to God.

But why do we need an external religion with all its rites, cults, ceremonies and the like? If we would keep to the teachings of the Spirit of God, then an external religion would be superfluous.

During past times God sent enlightened men, women and prophets to us, again and again. They never brought external religions, they also never built external institutions with cathedrals and church buildings; instead, they taught the inner religion, the religion of the heart. They explained to mankind about the two poles in the course of life, the before and after. But the external religions, which had no hold in themselves, therefore could also not offer their believers the hold that is in God in their inner being. They demanded and demand external, that is, tangible, concrete means that are to be found on the material, physical level, that is, priests, who then replace a lack of spiritual competence with shady moves filled with empty rites and ritualistic acts and talk about the alleged "mysteries of God."

Over the course of the centuries, the priests changed the truth of God according to their understanding and judgment. They narrowed down the encompassing knowledge about this side of life and the beyond, adapting it in their teachings to human desires and human needs, thus cutting to size and shaping the whole to be agreeable to the caste of priests, then and today, so as to keep every person who subjected himself to the external religion under their thumb. The people did this, partly out of ignorance and credulity, but often by relinquishing and sacrificing their reason, thus conforming themselves then and still today, imprisoned in the straightjacket of long, very long periods of indoctrination, and being weaned from independent, self-responsible thinking and living.

To be a theologian and a member of the clergy is to have an occupation and not a calling. The word clergy has little to do with the Spirit of God. The priest, the clergyman, is an office bearer in his church.

The power of the priests over their believers rests on the fact that the latter – through a monopolizing teaching and the ritualistic acts of the Church that supposedly are necessary for, and bring, salvation – appear to have no other possibility to understand and meet the challenges of their earthly existence on their own. They do not know where they come from and where they are going, and they do not know the law of sowing and reaping, of cause and effect.

An intrusion in the inner religion that brought the most serious consequences: The removal of reincarnation from the teachings of the wise and of the prophets

The most important and serious consequences brought about by the intrusion and break into the inner religion and the decisive step into a patriarchal thinking that exists only in a life on earth was taken when reincarnation was removed from the teachings of the wise and of the prophets. To this we can read the following in the Gabriele Letter 4:

In the year 553 at the Council of Constantinople, a majority vote condemned what the Early Christian teacher Origen had taught: that people's souls existed as spirit beings before their birth into a human body, and that the event of the Fall had led them into a state of physical existence. At the same time, they condemned the belief that all souls and humans would return to God one day. The council replaced this with the teaching of eternal damnation. And so, at that council, people rejected the teaching of Jesus of Nazareth: the message of a loving Father-God, who condemns no one to damnation, let alone eternally, but instead leads back all souls and people – with the help of the Redeemer-force of the Christ of God, which becomes effective by following His teachings. Also rejected was the knowledge about the pre-existence of the soul, one of the basic tenets of the teaching of reincarnation, which was also taught by Jesus of Nazareth, as we can see from several Early Christian writings. It is the teaching that is closely related to the law of sowing and reaping. The teaching of reincarnation lets us human beings understand why people in the western world have become as they are, as they present themselves today. People who could not comprehend the message of God, or did not want to – because their interests were not oriented to fulfilling the will of God – have distorted and changed the teachings from the Kingdom of God. The great wisdom of the conveyor of the message from heaven was forced into a narrow passage of incomprehensibility by those who indulge in self-adulation.

Over the course of centuries, the divine message was made more and more human and finally adapted to the desires and ambitions of the leaders of exter-nalized religion. These took the image of God and the law of God, including the law of reincarnation,

"What you sow today you will reap tomorrow or in a future incarnation," and pruned and cut it to shape and size so that it would fit what the religious leaders wanted. Because the watered-down teachings of the mainstream churches became ever more inconsistent and contradictory among themselves, the church "dignitaries" draped the guise of "mysteries of God" over them.

If in 553 at the Council of Constantinople, only a few of the spiritually unconscious had decided differently, the "mystery" would have been aired, and people in the western world would know all about the existence of the human soul before its physical embodiment and thus, about the basic tenets of the teaching of reincarnation.

This ill-starred decision robbed many people of the knowledge about the meaning and purpose of their life on earth. They no longer knew the inter-connections of their fate and did not know that the conditions for the birth of the soul into other worlds, into the beyond, depend on the behavior of the human being during his life on earth, all according to what the person thought, said and did. They also did not know that the return of the soul as a human being should be used to make amends for what the person had caused in former incarnations.

Let us realize that human beings even then – in 553 – were presumptuous enough to decide what is true and correct, and do so even today. When a church-goer asks about the "where from and where to," those who distorted the truth, the priests, cover it over with the mysteries of God, reasoning that: "God does not let just anyone see into His mysteries."

In its dimensions, the devastating consequences of this wrong decision can hardly be imagined.

Let us realize that the fatal consequences of this ignorance is that many think that their egotistical way of thinking and living, disparaging and dominating their fellowman, the torture, exploitation and murder of human beings and fellow creatures, the ruthless fight against the lives of others, the wanting to be and to have in its multitudinous variations etc., etc., etc. would merely bring them advantage and profit without punishment.

God never punishes. Man punishes himself, because he himself created the effects that he then – in this life on earth or in the soul realms or in future incarnations – has to experience on himself. Whoever always does the same and similar things against the law of freedom, against the eternal love, that is, whoever acts against the law of God with always the same thoughts and words, is heading toward a point where catastrophe begins for him: sorrow, illness or need.

But that is not everything; the disaster, which stems from spiritual ignorance, is far more extensive. Namely, that since the person does not know about the causal correlations of sowing and reaping, of cause and effect, a painful and sorrowful experience cannot, or can hardly, teach him anything, because he lacks the basic spiritual knowledge that is the basis for self-recognition. Instead of figuring out his own faults, his blame or partial blame, he usually places the blame solely on his neighbor, accusing, condemning and judging him, and thus increasing the weight of his own burden, instead of expiating some of it.

We know the path of probation, which is the path of self-recognition, of clearing things up and of doing them no more. There is also the path of expiation, which means to pay off guilt by suffering through what a person had done earlier to others. But without recognition of one's own wrong behavior, of one's own guilt, it is not possible to dissolve these negative energy potentials. But how shall a person recognize himself in the adversities he has experienced if he doesn't even know that he is the perpetrator himself, according to the law of sowing and reaping?

The result is that all the pain and suffering was endured for nothing, that all need and misery was suffered for nothing, if they did not lead to insight and to a change of ways. And so, much has been suffered in this world and in the soul realms, and still is!

We can see what terrible and far-reaching conse-quences the decision of 553 in Constantinople has for many, many people right up until today, and for the morals and ethics of private and public life! The Redeemer-power of the Christ of God can become effective only to a relatively low degree, because, for example, "faith alone is enough." With this, any spiritual knowledge, any experiences of God, any inner, religious life is declared superfluous, null and void. Ever since Constantinople, "Christian" is ultimately no longer Christian, but "Christendom" is a tool, an instrument in the hands of the opponent of God, the adversary, the darkness. (pp. 12-16)

And on pages 17-18 we read further:
The law of sowing and reaping that indicates to us the law of reincarnation is the justice of God and not last of all, His great love. It gives person and soul the chance to forgive and to make amends for unlawful deeds, in order to become free from the weight and burden that we have inflicted upon our souls. If our sinful aspects have been cleared up, our debt paid off, the result is that soul and person vibrate higher, because everything is radiation, vibration. Then, when the time of disembodiment comes, the soul can lightly and buoyantly return to the fine-material, eternal kingdom that is our eternal homeland.
And so, reincarnation, re-embodiment, gives the new human being a chance to make amends in this incarnation for the mistakes and faults he committed in former existences, that is, to even them out.

Not God led the people onto the wrong path,
but the caste of priests,
in order to bind the people to themselves

It was not God who led us onto the wrong path of ignorance and the "mysteries of God," but the caste of priests. The person who does not serve God, who does not serve the truth, who does not serve the life, who does not give the honor to Him alone and did not want to faithfully lead the sheep to the only Good Shepherd, Christ, instead seeking to serve his own honor, his own power, his own good living, and thus, the caste of priests, presumed to determine what may be considered truth.

Whoever has gotten out of the habit of thinking about the great totality, which is the truth, remains rooted in external religion, and everything that he cannot understand gets put into the ecclesiastical pigeonhole of "the mysteries of God." God never handed over the eternal truth to an intermediary; He never kept the truth to Himself. God gave us a total, a complete picture of heaven all the way to the earth and from the earth, in turn, to heaven.

Particularly in the western Christian world, the cosmic picture is lacking, the concept of the All, which is unity, equality, freedom, brotherliness and justice. By slashing the truth, by adapting to the practices and strivings of the human ego, through the ambition and will of the caste of priests, the external religion became a philosophical doctrine, an intellectual sophistry, from which no illuminating conclusions can be drawn about dying and about the beyond.

The caste of priests deliberately clouded and qualified the truth to serve their purposes and from this, they erected a dogmatic, traditional structure of ceremonies, to bind the people to them.

The building contractor of the structure of obfuscation, "church," clouded and darkened the truth, in order to relegate the love, the kindness, the forbearance and faithfulness of God to the realm of fairy-tales, to isolate the people from God, to even go so far as to incite the people against God, thus attributing the function of grace to themselves and securing the following of the faithful by keeping them dependent.

The truth is clear and basically simple. God is greatness. And the more simple it is to recognize the totality, the truth, the more we experience God's greatness. All of infinity is imbedded in the great unity of God. Whether we look at plants, animals or people, the essence of their existence is always the components of life; these are oriented toward unity. The Spirit is in every cell – whether in human beings, in plants or in the animals. We experience the components of the totality in all the organs of our physical body; it is the life. Depending on their consciousness, they form the unity in God, and every level of consciousness bears in itself the movement of life. Whether we think of the beating of a bird's wings, in which the power and the harmony of life become visible, or whether we think of the fish that move their fins, in everything, the basic pattern is recognizable, which means unity and in which evolution is an intrinsic part.

People need an encompassing view of the totality, which an external religion can never offer. To see life in its totality, the before and after, takes the fear of death from the one who does not rely on external religion but looks at the truth and at his own life from this standpoint. He knows what it means to die and that death is only a transition into a higher, lighter and more buoyant life, when the person truly – that means, consciously – has lived.

Many people go through their existence in despair. They escape into intemperance, into drugs and alcoholism, because they have fallen victim to the religious charlatans. These have darkened the meaning of life for them through their external religion and the maxim that faith alone is enough, so that for many, their existence on earth seems worthless. Whoever believes such religious comedians has lost the standard of his existence on earth.

If only you would become aware
of the greatness that lies in you!
The human being should bring to ripeness
the seed of his life, the core of being in him

If you have set out to take your life into your hands, then you will not run the danger of immediately entangling yourself in abstract concepts. Think about what greatness means. In the smallest, in the tiniest component of matter lies the greatness of the All. In the tiniest element, is reflected the eternal truth, creation, which is immortal.

125

Become aware of the fact that the Spirit is in all things. In you is the great Spirit of the cosmos. In your innermost being you are a being of infinity, a being of the All with the wonderful, immutable laws of the love for God and neighbor, the great unity, freedom and justice. Do not waste your earthly existence. Think about it; gain clarity over yourself, and from this follow the realizations that lie closest to your heart. You will experience that you are much greater in the Spirit than you can ever believe today.

But also become aware of the fact that the mortal person, the shell and the all-too-human aspects that mark the person, do not consist of the law of the Spirit. In the very basis of the soul, is the Spirit that keeps the human being alive. The human being, as such, is his own personal law. It is his earthly existence that is oriented toward the personal and the person, and that he should break down and recognize, in order to find his way to the truth.

The power of the Spirit in your soul is what I call the primordial power, the core of being or the seed of life. Every person is called to bring the primordial power, the core of being, the seed of his life, to maturity, with the power of the love for God and neighbor, with freedom, unity, with comprehension and understanding toward his fellowman, with honesty, openness and straightforwardness. Then we will gradually understand what life means and we will come to terms with death and dying, because the life that is in us grows. It is the very basis, the core of being, the seed of our true, eternal being, that makes us human beings lighter and freer, and sharpens our farsightedness and overview.

As often mentioned, nature gives us many hints; it is rooted in the Mother Earth. Every plant seed that lies in the earth can take root and grow in order to then attain full ripeness when the time has come. We, too, should be rooted in the Spirit and let the eternal Spirit work in and through us, just like the seed embedded itself in the Mother Earth and feels connected to the elements, in order to unfold from within and to fit into the great unity of all creation forms that fulfill His will, in honor of the Almighty, and in the way that is given to them from Him.

The pathway of the soul from the light all the way to becoming a human being in matter

Where do we come from and where are we going? Our pure spiritual body, the divine being that we are in God, came from the eternal light, from the life, the love, the purity, from the freedom, the kindness, from the Kingdom of God, the unending Being. A number of light-beings fell into a darkened state because they wanted to be like God and wanted to put themselves above God, so to speak. In this way, the spiritual particle structure of our divine body also became shadowed through the darkening of the light, for every one of us was once a being of light, which we eternally are in the very basis of our soul.

With increasing distance from God, the light-body of such a being successively became shadowed and, in the process of progressive change, which, among other things, also brought a densification, became a "soul." As the radiation continued to decrease, the former light-being, the soul, became a human being on the dwelling planet earth over the course of long cycles of energy. Later, much later, the possibility to procreate took shape. The male being, the man, procreated a shell, a new, small, human body, in the female being, the woman. On this very long cyclical pathway, it even came to serve the fine-material body, the soul, as a shell for its embodiment. During the course of the Fall that became ever deeper, the turning away from the light, the re-embodiment of the soul, called reincarnation, now very gradually began.

The "where to" of the human being – His task to return to his true origin

As long as a human being turns away from God, he always wants to be more than God. This leads to personal difficulties, to blows of fate, illness, need and loneliness, as well as to a lack of understanding toward his neighbor and his own earthly existence.

Dear friends, it is really a mistaken belief and particularly destructive to our earthly existence, when we think that we live solely in the temporal, and that then everything is over, that it is over for us. Why do we have a conscience, if everything is supposed to be over after this time on earth? Why are we often so dissatisfied when we do something that we recognize we shouldn't have done because it harms our fellowman and ourselves? These unbalanced rhythms in our earthly existence – the uncomfortable feeling of not having acted correctly – are the knocking of the Spirit of God in us. It is the life that is sending signals to our consciousness via our conscience, to warn us that what we are thinking, saying or doing is not in accordance with our true, eternal feeling of worthiness, the core of being, the seed of life in our soul.

God waits in us to reveal Himself to us. If we do not listen to God, the Eternal in us, the core of being, the seed, the very basis in our soul – by paying no attention to the Ten Commandments and the teachings of Jesus, the Christ – we will not understand the life either, and at the end of our earthly existence, we will not die in the awareness of life, but in the face of death. If we were spiritually dead as human beings, we will also be spiritually dead as souls; our soul will stay for a long time on the earth, because it is simply deeply rooted in the earth.

Our task as a human being is to bring our soul to full maturity, so that after passing on we may return as a divine being to the true origin of our being, to the Spirit of God in the Kingdom of God from where we went forth.

Only inner self-reliance leads to the dynamic life of the deed in the Spirit of God

Dear friends, take the time to analytically think about the "where from" and the "where to" and let your analytical thinking reverberate in your world of feelings. Then many a one will become aware, that he can figure out the roots of his eternal Being only when he has freed himself from bindings to people and to material assets.

This does not mean that we should withdraw into a hermit's existence. Quite the contrary! We should be in the midst of life on earth, fulfill our tasks, live with people, but not let ourselves become dependent on anything or anyone.

Think about the fact that every subjugation to an outside will, to the will of another, makes you passive and imposes a spiritual passivity on you.

A real life of the deed in the Spirit of God is possible only when it comes from inner self-reliance. For true creativity grows out of the inflow of divine power in one's own inner being. If the person maintains the connection to the primordial source of power, to the core of being of his soul, then God gives and is active through the person. His deeds will be fruitful for many.

Have you already thought about being useful? To be useful in the sense of the great totality, in the awareness of unity, in the knowledge that everything belongs together? If you want to, take on as a task to be useful up to an old age, which means, among other things, to recognize the unity, to preserve the unity, of which your fellowman, nature, the animals, the plants and the minerals are a part, yes, all of the cosmos. Then you will have a great task into your old age and you will always be among like-minded people, who want something similar, and do it, as you do.

Whoever learns this and also does it understands more and more what life is all about, what it means. For the person who is preoccupied less and less with his concerns, which are often very trivial, instead putting his life to work for God and for his fellowman, that is, who gives selflessly, will become free. Life opens up to him in ever deeper and finer nuances.

Through eyes and ears that are free from the noise and intoxication of the ego, we can see what others do not perceive. Through a sensitive hearing that is light-filled, we can hear what others do not understand. Through purified and free senses, we begin to fathom unity. Then we live in unity with people, animals and plants, with the Mother Earth, and we no longer do anything wrong in the garden of God, which Mother Earth wants to be for people, animals and nature.

Then the one or the other may very well say: This existence is worth living. And I say, that is life. That is the step-by-step return home into the Father's house.

*The bridge to God is the awareness
that has experienced the deep connection
between God, human being,
the nature kingdoms and the cosmos*

Our true return home to the Kingdom of God should
be brought to full maturity by us here in the temporal, for
Jesus said: *You shall be perfect, as your Father in heaven
is perfect.* This is possible only when we create the link
between God and ourselves, when we build this bridge on
which not only we walk, but on which we bring unity along
with us, the awareness that has experienced the deep
connection between God, human being, the nature kingdoms and the cosmos.

Whoever takes on the fulfillment of this task begins to
live and feels the lightness of his own soul. The one who
affirms the great creation in matter and in the whole universal cosmos, who orients himself to the rules of life of the
eternal laws, of love, freedom and unity, finds the way
upward into the light, because his soul becomes lighter
and the person can recognize what unity, equality, freedom,
brotherliness and justice signify.

Whoever works himself into these great creation
thoughts of love, unity, equality, freedom, brotherliness
and justice through a meaningful analysis with heart and
mind also understands what God wants.

God does not want each one to close himself off from
the other. God wants a great nation of people who do His
will. Do not become negligent in meaningful analysis,

for every one has to recognize at some point what God wants. For every soul, this is unavoidable. Every soul has to sooner or later find its way again to freedom and attain unity, for the body of light is immortal and is all-cosmic law. By way of unqualified analysis, we become a good observer who doesn't simply accept everything that others want to make us believe.

We should be aware of the fact that no person can leave his life up to others, not to an external religion, either. Every person is called on by the great Spirit to refine himself, to ennoble his character. So that we achieve this, we have God's wisdom in His commandments and in the teachings of the Sermon on the Mount of Jesus, the Christ. Today, we are offered the whole, widely diversified spectrum of highest divine teachings in ever new variations, applicable in the daily life of the individual, accessible for any person in countless books, on tape and on CDs, in transmissions and radio broadcasts all over the earth.

And so, we have teachings upon teachings from the divine Being, help upon help from the Kingdom of God. Do not leave your life up to the analysis of science and theology. You yourself are asked; you yourself can do a meaningful analysis in order to fathom yourself in the depths, in order to draw closer to your eternal being step by step and in the light of the truth and, in your surroundings, to learn to distinguish between appearance and Being. As long as a person is unfree, he relates everything to himself and bends everything according to his will, according to his criteria and thus, according to his level of consciousness.

Between sowing and reaping
lies the time of ripening, during which
we can recognize and pay off our causes
here in a life on earth before the effects set in

Today, we human beings are placed in a time that is a powerful time of radical change, and that gives us reason to think about ourselves more intensely, to shed light on our life on earth in order to feel and sense who we are in terms of our origin, where we come from and where we are going.

The one who distances himself from his narrow concept of living only in the temporal senses that everything that he sees or even does not see is in interaction with him. Ultimately, every soul and every person is woven into this interaction, as well as the Mother Earth and everything that lives on, over and in her. When we ignore the truth, when we push it away from us, we can chase as much as we want after life, after fulfillment of life, after our happiness, and accumulate for ourselves and our future so much seemingly secure material things – nonetheless we will always remain unhappy and anxious, because we have placed ourselves to the left of the truth.

Whoever strives to get to the bottom of the truth understands the following saying: *"Just as you call into the canyon, that is how it echoes back,"* and, *"Whoever doesn't want to listen will have to feel."* These statements help us realize that there is a direct interaction, and that we cannot call something into the canyon that will then sound back to us as an echo but with a different content. Whatever goes out from us in feelings, thoughts, words and actions, that is, what we store in our soul, comes back to us – light or shadow, lightness or heaviness.

Particularly in nature we can recognize the perfection of God. Nature can be externally changed by us human beings, but the inner being, the spiritual substance, remains the same. When we externally change the conditions in nature, when we reshape, pollute, violate or maltreat it for our own self-serving purposes, this violation, this offence against God's creation, will come back to us. Even the climate change is proof of the law, "What a person sows he will reap." Who gave rise to the climate change? The Spirit of unity, or the human being, through the destruction on and in the Mother Earth, through his influence on the atmosphere and so very much more? The human being has declared war on nature, and thus, on the earth. But today one can already see that the loser is the human being.

The Fall-thought of wanting to be like God or even more means that the earth and the world have to be changed and that even God's creation has to be improved upon. But God's law is unalterable. That which is perfect is not capable of improvement. Every negative change in one's personal life on and in the earth hits back at the author at some point. In the long run, no person can oppose the perfection of God and His eternal law of unity. Whoever nevertheless does this, will be shipwrecked at some point and suffer under it. What we are now experiencing in our

135

world, also in the climate change, is nothing more than the repercussion of what man himself has caused.

Only the person who lives according to the All-law of love, freedom and unity is free. The grace of God and His help, about which the caste of priests make too many words, lie between the cause and the effect, between the seed and the harvest. When we produce causes, that is, when we sow negativity, we will not immediately reap the harvest. Between sowing and reaping, a certain leeway exists, which we could call the phase of ripening. During this "time of ripening," the help of God and the offer of His hand is always granted to us. But this time between, however, is not unlimited. Nature also teaches this to us. When the fruit has ripened, the harvest takes place. Then the corresponding effect follows the cause, the negative harvest, the negative seed.

Insightful learning helps us to work our way out of the shadows, out of the heaviness, into the light. But whoever began a wrong development and accelerated it by always thinking and doing the same, that is, by always watering the negative seed with negativity, is inevitably heading toward a point where disaster, the negative harvest, cannot be avoided.

As mentioned, the law of cause and effect has a certain predetermined leeway that lies in the cause, in the corresponding seed. If we do not learn to recognize our causes in good time, sooner or later we fall into our effects, which may drive us to reincarnate after our earthly death, that is, to again be born in the flesh.

Our earthly life is set up in such a way that we can undo the negativity, the wrongdoing against the life, here in the coarse-material, in the temporal, and not first in the fine-material, in the purification planes, once our soul has released itself from its body.

Life on earth is valuable! We should often make ourselves aware of this. Every mistake that we make is countered by the corresponding life-affirming forces and virtues that we are able to unfold by way of affirmation and fulfillment. Which forces we allow to become effective always depends on us.

The signs of the times cannot be overlooked.
Each one must ask himself whether
he is not also responsible for
the disaster of our world today.
Each one can decide each day:
For or against God

Whoever observes the present world with alert senses must perceive with shock that man cannot, in the long run and unlimitedly, remain a remorseless disruptor of the harmony of creation. The signs of the times cannot be overlooked. God draws a very long breath, because He loves His children. But we should not forget that God's mills grind slowly, but surely. God does not allow Himself to be mocked. What a person sows he will reap.

During our time, each one is asked to restrain himself and to make a touchstone of his own thinking, speaking and doing. Based on the law of cause and effect, no one can wriggle out of it and say "the other one is to blame!" Each one has to seriously ask himself whether he, too, doesn't carry a part of the guilt for the disaster of our world today. The decision of each one is asked, and not passing the blame to others.

Today, every day, we should decide: for or against God, for the law of the All, for the freedom – or for the personal law which so marks the world, the ego-law of the yoke, the binding, the suffering, fate, illness, need, and perhaps includes a horrible death.

Life, in order to die in the face of life and then continue on living, or death, which is the same as spiritual blindness, are basic in their differences. Every person must die. But his soul doesn't have to be spiritually dead. To die means to slip into the beyond and into the fine-material life. To be dead means to be spiritually dead, to be unawakened, to not recognize life as such. To be dead also means to be near the earth. Whoever has merely languished through life in the face of death is afraid, and fear always has torment in its wake.

Life is God, and whoever fulfills the will of God lives. He will neither taste nor feel death.

Dear friends, when the course of our existence on earth completes its circle, we should not go away with empty hands and empty hearts, but go with a rich and God-conscious life's harvest. A rich life's harvest bears wonderful character traits. Nothing that is truly good dies – it goes into the light of eternity.

The one who uses the time of harvest, acts wisely in order to unearth the true treasure, the treasure of the inner being, and multiply it by giving the best that comes from God, and strives to give inner joy. Who truly unearths the treasure of life, keeps it during his days on earth and beyond death. And when the circle of his existence on earth has closed, his good works will continue to live in the beyond, just as his soul will go into the light-filled spheres of life because the works of his life were good.

Our life should be a refuge, Bethlehem, filled with God-pleasing thoughts and works of life.

Books in the Universal Life Series

This Is My Word –
A and Ω – The Gospel of Jesus
The Christ Revelation,
which true Christians the world over have come to know

A book that lets you really get to know about Jesus, the Christ, about the truth of his activity and life as Jesus of Nazareth. From the contents: The falsification of the teachings of Jesus of Nazareth during the past 2000 years - Jesus loved the animals and always spoke up for them - Meaning and purpose of a life on earth - Jesus taught about marriage - God is not a wrathful God - The teaching of "eternal damnation" is a mockery of God - Life after death - Equality between men and women - The coming times and the future of mankind, and much more!

1078 pages / Order No. S 007en, ISBN: 978-1-890841-17-1

The Word of the Christ of God –
To Mankind Before This World Passes Away
Nearer to God in You

Believe, trust, hope and endure! What do these mean and how can we apply them on our way to God? How do we turn belief into an active faith? How do we develop trust? Hope is expressed in setting goals that are carried out with confidence. What does it mean to endure in the divine sense? Experience the Inner Path in condensed form. Simple clear words, given to all people who long for God and a fulfilled, happy life in freedom. A gift from God to all His human children.

112 pages / Order No. S 139en, ISBN: 978-1-890841-45-4

God Heals

There is a mighty, indescribable power in us. It is the central power of love, God's power and healing. Learn how this power in you can be unfolded!

61 pages / Order No. S 309en, ISBN: 978-1-890841-23-2

The Path to Cosmic Consciousness –
Happiness, Freedom and Peace

The path to cosmic consciousness is the path to inner happiness and inner peace, to the feeling of having "arrived." Where? In the Kingdom of God, of which Jesus, the Christ, already taught, that it can be found within, in every person. It is our true, divine being. This is a path of liberation, which Gabriele, the prophetess and messenger of God, walked ahead of us. As a guide, she showed how we can learn not only to fulfill our work more quickly and conscientiously, but also how we can make peace with our fellowman and with nature and the animals, and how we can maintain it. Through this, we become happy and free!

75 pages / Order No. S 341en, ISBN: 978-1-890841-60-7

The Sermon on the Mount –
Life in Accordance With the Law of God

Timeless instructions for a peaceful and fulfilled life. A path that leads the way out of the dead-end in which so many people find themselves today. An excerpt from a work of revelation "This Is My Word."

112 pages / Order No. S 008en, ISBN: 978-1-890841-42-3

Live the Moment –
and You Will See and Recognize Yourself

Now, in this instant, the state of our soul shows itself. We can see it in our feelings, thoughts, words and actions that take place at every moment in us. Become sensitive to the signals of your inner life...

76 pages / Order No. S 315en, ISBN: 978-1-890841-54-6

Where Did I Come From? Where Am I Going?

The wherefrom and whereto of our life is no longer a mystery. Following explanations of the important questions on life after death, answers are given to the 75 most frequently asked questions on this topic.

75 pages / Order No. S 407en, ISBN: 978-1-890841-54-6

Cause and Development of All Illness
What a person sows, he will reap

A book more relevant than ever before, more exciting than a thriller, more moving than a documentary ... Many details revealed over 20 years ago by the Spirit of God are confirmed today by science: Without a healthy, balanced relationship between human beings, animals, plants and minerals, mankind will not survive in the long run. What does this mean for the future? What are the effects of man's destructive behavior toward nature, the animals and, not least, his own state of health? Learn about until now unknown correlations and frontier zones between spirit and matter, about the effect of the power of thoughts on our life, for instance, how harmful parasites and pathogens can be created by our behavior patterns, about holistic healing, the meaning of life on earth, and much more ...

360 pages / Order No. S 117en, ISBN: 978-1-890841-37-9

The Message From the All

NEW!
God does not forsake mankind, His children. He again speaks His direct word through His prophetess, giving answers to the basic questions of mankind, particularly in relation to the spiritual correlations that are not explained in the Bible: on the meaning and purpose of a life on earth, the freedom of every person, Christ's deed of redemption, the infinite love of God for every person and all of creation and much, much more.

For over 30 years, the All-Spirit, God, has been giving mankind His word in countless revelations through Gabriele, His prophetess and messenger. From the great treasure of these divine revelations, 14 have been selected and published for the first time.

The light of eternal truth shines into our time and the events of our time, so that each one, who opens his heart to the message of God, may recognize what God has to say to him, and, if he wants to, apply it in his life.

187 pages / Order No. S 137en, ISBN: 978-1-890841-36-2

To order any of these books or to obtain a complete catalog of all our books, please contact:

Gabriele Publishing House
P.O. Box 2221, Deering, NH 03244
(844) 576-0937
WhatsApp/Messenger: +49 151 1883 8742
www.Gabriele-Publishing-House.com

or:

THE WORD
P. O. Box 5643
97006 Wuerzburg
GERMANY

www.universal-spirit.org
e-mail: info@universelles-leben.org

or:
You can also order our books at: Amazon.com